CONTEMPLATING LIFE
FROM THE BACK STEP

CONTEMPLATING LIFE FROM THE BACK STEP

A story of life lessons learned from three slightly crazy Boxer dogs

Angela Lemanis

Library of Congress Control Number:		2012922998
ISBN:	Hardcover	978-1-4797-6016-9
	Softcover	978-1-4797-6015-2
	Ebook	978-1-4797-6017-6

This book is a work of nonfiction based on the life, experiences, and recollections of the author.

To order additional copies of this book, contact:
Xlibris Corporation
0800-891-366
www.xlibris.co.nz
Orders@Xlibris.co.nz
700420

FOR MY FAMILY:

Andrej, Marie, Peter, Damian, and my buddy Jen.
In memory of my beautiful boxer dogs.

CONTENTS

ACKNOWLEDGEMENTS

I HAVE NOT BEEN alone when it came to writing this book. I started writing it with no real idea of what I would do with it at the end. This journey began because I wanted to document all of the funny stories that I remembered about Towser, Sammie, and Max. Because Towser was my first experience with the boxer breed and because I was a teenager when I'd had the bulk of those experiences, I was terrified that I'd forget them as I got older. The only times I found myself talking openly about Towser was with Mum, Dad, and my brother Damian; and they'd often retell stories that I had forgotten. The same went for Sammie. I wanted to capture all the times he made me laugh, worry, cry, and the times that he made me proud. These two dogs were such exceptionally beautiful personalities that I wanted to commit my memories of them to paper so that I could remember them when I grew old. Max was essentially the catalyst for getting my butt in gear. When I got Max, I was so surprised to see how many character traits he shared with Towser and Sammie. All of the same quirky behaviours were surfacing again, and to my pleasant surprise, more were coming out of the woodwork every day. So much so that I commented to my husband Andrej that I actually thought Max might be the reincarnation of Sammie.

So one rainy afternoon, I started documenting the stories. It struck me that if my boxers were all relatively similar, then other boxer dog owners might recognise their dog's personality in some of the stories and be able to relate. The book grew from there as I expanded it to not only capture the stories of my boxers, but also the lessons they taught me through their wonderful natures.

Even as the book grew and developed, I still didn't think it would really ever see the light of day. Andrej was the only one in those early days that I shared the chapters with. It was during a conversation he had quite by accident one day with a publisher friend that a turning point occurred. That friend was Geoff Blackwell, who told Andrej that he'd be happy to read over my manuscript and provide honest advice. I freaked out when I heard this because now I had to set "it" free and see if someone else thought it had any substance. That changed the way I viewed my manuscript and planted the seed in my mind that this could actually go somewhere. So thank you, Geoff, for your sound advice and enthusiastic honesty. I might never have had the courage to see this through if it hadn't been for you.

Special thanks go to my fantastically wonderful husband Andrej for always supporting me and for having a steadfast and unwavering faith in me. He could see how passionate I was about this and was always gentle in his honesty and encouragement. Thanks for being as caring and loving of Max as I am and for having such patience in those crazy puppy years. I love you biggest and most of all and could not have done this without you.

A debt of gratitude also goes to my mum Marie and dad Peter for reading through the chapters and providing much-needed feedback. Some of my memories were hazy, and they helped to provide the accuracy to the details. Thanks also to my parents for introducing me to the boxer breed and for finally giving in to my numerous pleas to get a dog. Recognition should probably also go to their first boxer, Ben, for being such a lovely dog that they considered another boxer when I begged for a puppy. They couldn't have known that first day we had Towser that he—and the boxers that followed him—would be so inspiring to me that they'd prompt a book.

I'm also very appreciative to my brother Damian, my friend Jenny, and all of my Aussie and Kiwi friends who have been my cheerleaders—thanks for the heartfelt encouragement, support, and care.

To Chief, you didn't get a mention in the book, but life at home with Andrej, Max, and I wouldn't be the same without you. Thanks for being a quiet, serious, and resilient friend to us all. We love you!

Life Lessons Learned from My Boxers

L ET ME BEGIN by saying that this is not a self-help book. I am always surprised when I go into a bookstore and find so many self-help books on the shelf. It seems that as a species, we humans need lots of help to live our lives—or should I say, to live our lives in a healthy, well-adjusted way. Dogs don't have this problem. I discovered this fact after carefully observing my boxer dogs and how they spent their days. My dogs seemed to instinctively know how to enjoy themselves and to fill their days savouring each and every moment. Having dedicated time to watching my dogs, I noticed that certain features were true of every dog I've owned. These features seemed to be universal regardless of each individual dog's appearance, personality, temperament, and quirks. It's almost as if my dogs knew things I didn't or paid attention to the things I should have.

This book is essentially the tale of three slightly crazy boxer dogs and the lessons I've learned through watching them and the natural laws that govern their lives. It is surprising when, where, and from whom you learn life's lessons and timing is everything; the exact point in time that the lesson presents itself coupled with the exact point in your life that you're ready to learn. I have learned so many fundamental lessons from my mum and dad but the lessons in this book are the life lessons from the dogs in my life. Probably the only reason I paid attention to these is because of my sheer love of the boxer dog breed.

The idea for this book came from watching one of my boxers, Max, sit on the top step of our back deck every night at around the same time, sniffing the air and listening to the sounds of the neighbourhood. Like all of the boxer dogs in my life have done, Max sat with his bottom on the higher step and his front paws on the step below. I would stand quietly in the kitchen as he sat out there, his back to me and his nose elevated in the night air. I marvelled at this little bit of quiet time he stole for himself every night and wondered, *What's he thinking about?* I joked to my husband that Max was out there "contemplating life," and we'd laugh and leave him to it. One night, I went out and joined him. The two of us sat there side by side, looking out into the backyard and listening to the sounds of the neighbour's chatter and savouring the dinner smells that would waft past our noses at regular intervals. Sitting quietly next to my dog in the cool evening air was calming and peaceful, and I understood in that second why he would make a point of doing this every night. As we sat there in silence, he gently leaned into me. He didn't move his paws or anything; he just leaned in so that our sides were touching. And there we sat for a good while, just enjoying the time together. It was as if he'd let me in on his little secret.

As you've probably gathered, I am a self-confessed, unabashed "dog person." I believe that all dogs are wonderful creatures and a true blessing to the owners who are graced by their presence and love. But having said that, I must also divulge that I am unashamedly biased towards the boxer dog breed. There's just something remarkably special about the boxer dog.

The boxer's zest for life (and everything in it) means that they are frequently described as the clowns of the canine community. This is true! Just as there is a touch of madness in every genius, there is a touch of crazy in every boxer. I am sure that if you examined the DNA structure of a boxer dog, you would find the standard physical characteristics of floppy ears, wrinkles, springy legs, and soulful brown eyes entwined with a temperament of good naturedness, a healthy sense of wonderment, and a contagiously buoyant spirit.

As the 1938 American Kennel Club Boxer Breed Standard states, "The character of the Boxer is of the greatest importance and demands the most solicitous attention. He is renowned from olden times for his great love and faithfulness to his master and household. He is harmless in the family, but distrustful of strangers, bright and friendly of temperament at play, but brave and determined when aroused. His intelligence and willing tractability, his modesty and cleanliness make him a highly desirable family dog and cheerful companion. He is the soul of honesty and loyalty, and is never false or treacherous even in his old age."

I have known three boxers over the course of my thirty-nine years: Towser, Sampson (Sammie), and Max—all tan and white male boxer dogs. Each one has popped into my life and imparted their knowledge and pearls of doggie wisdom at times when I've needed it most. As a spiritual person, I believe that my boxers have been my guides, sharing their special kind of insight and teaching me such important character traits as patience, perseverance, and resourcefulness. The way in which they have imparted these life lessons is unique, to say the least, but there's no mistaking that each lesson was cloaked in affection and dispensed with boundless energy.

But first things first. You've got to meet my boxer dogs.

LESSON 1

A Stranger Will Change Your Life

E VERY PERSON IN our lives today was once a stranger. As Shakespeare wrote in his play *As You Like It*, "All the world's a stage, and all the men and women merely players: they have their exits and their entrances . . ." Everybody that enters our lives does so for a reason whether that is to help us, support us, guide us, raise us, befriend us, or educate us. Every person has a role to play and their own special brand of wisdom to share. My three boxer dogs were once strangers until those three fateful moments when their paths crossed mine, and they changed my life forever. The first boxer to do this was Towser.

Towser

Towser and I met one Friday afternoon—he, a little bundle of tan-and-white fur, and I, a thirteen-year-old in my school uniform. Mum collected me from school, and off we went to the breeder's place to pick up Towser and bring him home to join my dad and my older brother Damian in our family. I was so excited to be getting my first dog. I had always wanted one and pestered my parents until I thought I could pester no more. My parents were not newcomers to the boxer breed as they'd had a lovely boxer named Ben when they were first married. Growing up, every time I heard my parents talk about Ben, it was prefaced with Beautiful Ben. He had been a great addition to their new life together, and photo albums are filled with images of him staring intently at the camera, head tilted to the side, tongue hanging out, and eyes full of mischievous curiosity. His time with my parents was filled with great adventures but, unfortunately, was not long enough. He had been purchased from a local pet shop, and in those days, there weren't the thorough health checks done on puppies when you bought them. Big beautiful Ben was sick, and after two fleeting years on earth, my parents had the heartbreaking task of taking him to the vet one last time. He had left his mark though—his presence in their lives, though brief, made a lasting impression and left enduring memories that they still laugh about today.

It was the way that my parents talked about him that made me want to have a dog of my own. Ben was the benchmark, and it took them a while to grieve him and to be ready to open their heart to another dog. But after fifteen years, the time had come. As a family, it was debated as to whether getting another boxer would be tempting fate; would we get another boxer as lovely as Ben was? Eventually it was decided that yes, if we were going to have a dog join our family unit, it should be a boxer. So there I was in the car, brimming with excitement, on the way to get our new puppy Towser.

I had visions of him sleeping on my bed, following me around the house, and just generally being *my* dog, but I was soon to discover that Towser had his own thoughts on what he should be doing at any given moment. I was also soon to discover that the words *headstrong* and *naughty* would be used repeatedly and often when describing our new furry family member!

From the moment I bent down and gathered Towser up into my arms and looked into his big brown eyes, I was sold. From that point on, I was destined to be a fan of the boxer dog. The whole way home, I managed to keep a clutching hold on him while he wriggled, licked my face, chewed on my fingers with his piranha-like puppy teeth and stayed in a constant state of exaggerated motion. He had that puppy smell about him (a mixture of milk and puppy food) and breathed in excited little *hah, hah, hah* breaths. His tail had been docked soon after birth (this was the '80s), and even though he was only ten weeks old and his stumpy tail only about fifteen centimetres long, he waggled it like there was no tomorrow. So much so, that every time he wagged it, his entire rear end got the wriggles and moved energetically from side to side. It looked like some strange dance he was trying to perform.

Towser took to life with our family well. After getting home, meeting everyone, and giving them the cursory once over, he fell into a deep sleep. How cute he was—all tiny and pudgy with his soft fur, floppy ears, and big paws. Sitting with him while he slept, I was determined to get my parents' approval for him to sleep in my room that first night. They'd already arranged a little wooden box for him with a soft wool blanket and a chew toy. It was positioned near a loudly ticking clock that the breeder had suggested we use to help him sleep as it would remind him of his mother's heartbeat. I, however, was thinking that he could sleep on my bed, and I would be there in case he woke up and got scared. While contemplating my plan for this, I was greeted with a symphony of smells and sounds. First, it was the noxious gas emanating from his rear end (something that I have since learned is a common boxer affliction), followed by a series of high-pitched grumbles, grunts, wheezes, and snores. I couldn't believe so many sounds could come from such a tiny creature and that these sounds could emit from each end simultaneously. I was quickly rethinking the "let him sleep with me" strategy. The little box didn't look so bad after all!

From that first night with Towser, my life changed. In a matter of hours, I had gone from never having a dog to loving this one so much I couldn't imagine not having him. He brought an energy to the house that was so infectiously cheery and playful, it was hard not to be affected by it.

I noticed that as a family, we were all getting up a little bit earlier so that we could catch some extra time alone with him before heading off to work or school. I would come down to the breakfast room to find my dad sitting on the floor playing with him, or my mum sneaking a quiet little conversation in while he sat at her feet waiting for breakfast. He, of course, was intently listening to every word she said while his little nose worked overtime sniffing the air. I'd never seen my parents interact with a puppy before, so it was funny to hear my mum talking to him like a baby and to see Dad wrestling with him and laughing at his puppy playfulness. Until now, we had all been busy with our work and school routines, and now we had a new family member who demanded our attention. We loved it.

Towser wasn't my cuddliest boxer. He wasn't a big fan of cuddles, but he did like to have at least one part of himself touching you if you were in his general vicinity. If Mum and Dad were standing together in the kitchen, Towser would always position himself to be standing in between them. If Dad was sitting on the floor with the Sunday paper spread out, Towser would be sitting right beside him with his paw either on Dad or on the paper. If you were standing beside Towser and he was sitting, he'd lean onto your leg. He was affectionate, but in an understated way and always on his terms. He was such a beautiful dog, and I was always amazed at how much I could immediately love a dog that had just come into my life. He lived a largely relaxed life in the tropics of North Queensland before saying his final farewell to us at the age of ten and a half years.

Sammie

The second boxer to change my life was Sampson or, as my parents and I came to call him, Sammie. I was twenty and had just returned from living overseas in Canada. After finding a job and an apartment in the same town where my parents lived, I decided that I wanted to have a little boxer puppy to look after. Around the same time, my parents were approached by Towser's vet to see if they would agree to him breeding his female boxer dog

ANGELA LEMANIS

Roxy with Towser. Towser was about seven years of age at the time—and this might have been his only opportunity to breed—so my parents agreed, and Towser and Roxy met and spent the weekend together. Not long after, the vet told us that Roxy was pregnant and that we could have one of the puppies when they were born. Sammie was that puppy.

From the moment I picked him up from the vet's place, I knew I had a kindred spirit with me. Sammie was one of two surviving puppies. Roxy had had a litter of seven, but due to problems feeding them, only two had survived: Sammie and his sister. I knew that I wanted a male dog rather than a female one so the choice was easy. Both of them had plenty of energy and were just so adorable. The ten minutes I spent sitting on the ground with them at the vet's property while they ran over my legs, chewed on my shoe, and barked at me were the most wonderfully hectic. Their collective enthusiasm was contagious, and I couldn't help but feel excited about the whole deal too. After deciding that I was going to take Sammie, I got his documents from the vet and gave him one last chance to say good-bye to his sister and mum Roxy. Obviously, he wasn't aware of what was about to happen, but I think that Roxy knew because as I headed towards the car with Sammie in my arms; Roxy followed closely behind. When I got into the car and closed the door, Roxy jumped up onto the car door and looked in at me through the window. She knew that I was taking Sammie away from her, and the confused look on her face almost broke my heart. At least she had the sister puppy to look after, but I still felt a pang of guilt as my parents started the car and drove down the long driveway of the vet's property. Sammie, of course, was none the wiser as his full attention was focused on chewing the strap of my seatbelt.

Being one of the surviving puppies, Sammie was strong and a good eater (something that stayed consistent throughout his life). That first night, I gave him some puppy food, and he attacked it with such fervour that I knew my new puppy was a canine epicurean greedy-guts! I stood nearby watching him while he practically inhaled that first meal in his new home, and I could visibly see his stomach expanding. He resembled a miniature cow—short legs but a stomach that was almost round. During those first few days, I noticed that Sammie was a very independent character and happy to investigate things on his own. He had a whole new world to become acquainted with, and he seemed to be wasting no time. His weakness was that he could only manage to be on the go for a few hours at a time before he needed to recharge his young batteries with a power nap.

Sammie was more affectionate than Towser, and he would let you hug him for as long as you wanted to. He liked being near others and would often come and sit beside you or sleep at your feet. When Sammie was older (around twelve years of age), my husband and I were moving to New Zealand for his job. I wanted to take Sammie with us, but he was visibly old and had a touch of arthritis. I was worried that the colder New Zealand weather would cause him multiple problems as would the change of location, house, and schedule. It was decided that he would stay in sunny North Queensland with my parents rather than put him through a big life change at his age. I missed him terribly but went back often enough to visit him (and my parents, of course). He loved staying with my parents, and I had the peace of mind that he was being incredibly well looked after as they loved him just as much as I did. When I did go back to visit, Sammie—who usually slept outdoors on the veranda—would come and sleep on the ground outside my bedroom window. It was almost as if he wanted me to know that he was just on the other side of the bedroom wall. I could hear him breathing and snoring, and most nights I would sneak a peek at him as he lay there sleeping. Sammie was a very special dog—a lovely soul. He died at the ripe old age of thirteen and a half years, which is not a bad age for a boxer dog. Mum and Dad were with him at the end and said that while it was very sad to see him go, the experience for Sammie seemed a peaceful one.

Max

ANGELA LEMANIS

My third and current boxer is Max, and I got him in New Zealand. He became otherwise known in our household as Mad Max. *Mad* as in totally wacky. My husband and I were living in Auckland, and we had been debating about whether to get a dog as it had been almost three years since Sammie died.

After doing much research regarding breeders on the North Island, we decided to look at three puppies from a breeder in Hamilton (about two hours drive south of Auckland). Two weeks before the Easter break, I drove down to the breeder to have a look at the litter and to select my new puppy. Approaching the breeder's property, I saw a nice, modern house on a semi-rural property; and from the outside, the house had a serene, peaceful quality to it. I parked out the front, jumped out of the car, and inhaled the fresh country air as I approached the front door. Talk about calm before the storm! After not having a dog for a while and not having had a puppy in nearly seventeen years, I had forgotten what it was that I was getting myself into.

After greeting the ever-so-slightly frazzled-looking breeder and entering the house, it was as if I had been transported into a parallel universe—a chaotic world filled with poopy footsteps, irregularly formed puddles, a flurry of fur, ears, and legs scurrying every which way, and high-pitched *ruff ruff* sounds. The energy radiating out from these little boxers was palpable. There were several plump puppies scampering around on the floor. Each footstep I took was fraught with the danger of accidentally stepping on one of them as they scooted in and out between my feet. My little Max was known as Spot then because he had a tiny white spot on the back of his otherwise reddy-brown neck fur. There were eight puppies altogether, but five of them were already spoken for. From the three remaining puppies I could choose from, I noticed that Spot/Max had gravitated towards me. He seemed to be studying me as much as I was watching them. While the other two puppies greeted me with momentary curiosity, they soon left to do their own thing while Max stayed in my general vicinity—not too close but never far away either. Every now and then he'd venture over and check out my shoes or look up at me with a waggle of his tiny tail. I picked him up so that we were at eye level with each other, and he immediately jerked forward and licked my face. Yep, he was the one. I could come back in two weeks' time to take him home.

So there I was on collection day, which also happened to be Good Friday. Mum was flying in from Australia that night to spend the Easter holidays with me as my husband Andrej was away for work. I made the drive down in the morning with a friend from work. She had agreed to come along for the trip so that she could hold Max on the return journey. We arrived at the breeder's place and again walked into a noisy reception. The breeder—still looking frazzled—wasted no time scooping Max up off the floor and handing him to me with one hand while presenting me with his puppy information pack and a discount voucher for 10 percent off premium puppy food with the other. One minute and $800 later, I was the proud owner of an eight-week-old puppy and being shown the door. The breeder finally smiled as I said good-bye and walked to the car as the thought of one less puppy running around her house dawned on her. That's when reality set in. The two-hour drive home was going to be interesting with a creature that seemed to be jacked up on a caffeine high. Thankfully, ten minutes into the drive, Max ran out of juice and proceeded to sleep the entire way home. He was happy to be curled up on my friend's lap with his new doggie blanket (which was actually a fleece baby blanket I bought at a baby store) to snuggle into. When Mum arrived that night, she was anxious to meet Max. He enjoyed having another person showering him with love and attention. Over the course of a couple of days, Mum and I noticed that five minutes or so before he fell asleep, Max would have a crazy fit of energy and just go "mad", chew on things, run around, or bark loudly. We termed it his Mad Max moment. Five minutes later, he'd collapse blissfully in an exhausted heap sound asleep.

You will learn more about each of these wonderful boxer dogs throughout the chapters of this book. I have always cherished the changes that have occurred with the addition of each of my boxers and have also learnt that most times, change is good. But I didn't always feel this way. It took a lesson from Towser to get me on track.

LESSON 2

Change Isn't All Bad

AMERICAN ACTRESS MEG Ryan once said about change, "People are always telling me that change is good. But all that means is that something you didn't want to happen has happened." This quote resonated strongly with me when I was younger as my adolescent mind perceived the negative aspects of change only—a door had closed on something I was familiar with. This view wasn't tempered with the more balanced stance that other doors may open in its place. I would lament the loss of what I had known and couldn't see the new opportunities awaiting me. As time has passed and I've experienced more change in my life, I've come to accept that change is not the exception. It's inevitable, and ultimately, it's all about how you respond to it that makes the difference in your perception of it.

When my husband and I moved to Auckland for his work, I thought that a change of scene and a change in lifestyle might be exciting—a new adventure of sorts—as we'd lived in our previous place for seven years. Beginning my working life in Auckland in a government public relations department coincided with a period of time when words like *restructure*, *transition*, and *amalgamation* were bandied around like punch lines in some ill-timed, nonhumorous corporate joke. For the staff, it seemed that as soon as you became comfortable with your role and your place in the organisation, they announced some kind of change. It would start insignificantly enough with a change to your job title. This was followed by the downsizing of your team or mergers with other similarly sized teams. Then before you knew it, entire groups were reviewed and restructured. The organisation I was working for had ticked "yes, please" to all of the previous steps and topped it off by amalgamating with seven other organisations to become a new "super organisation" (or at least that's how the media referred to it). In my experience, reality was a lot less super.

This constant state of flux became annoying and unsettling, mostly because the change management process was ineffective in its implementation.

This indirection only served to leave the majority of employees fearing the future. I found it situationally ironic that the organisation's management tried to put a spin on it (to a group of professional spin doctors!) by saying the change was an "opportunity" to find efficiencies and improvements. This little gem of wisdom was wheeled out at every available meeting, presentation, and staff newsletter; so much so, that I thought I might throttle the next person who regurgitated this little nugget of management wisdom. It was really just code for reducing head count and merging two workloads into one. If you survived the restructure, you found yourself not only doing your original job, but also the job of your former colleague who had been "let go." Twice the work, same pay—now there's efficiency if ever I saw it! (Sarcasm much?)

While the untimely change was a top-down directive from the "powers that be", it was enough of a jolt to make me stop and consider the wider picture: Am I where I want to be? Am I doing what I want to do now that I'm in my thirty-somethings? The answer was a resounding *no*.

I had studied journalism at university and completed a postgraduate certificate in public relations. And whilst that had been the path I wanted to follow when I was in my twenties, in my thirties, I found myself primarily involved in issue identification, risk assessment, and crisis management for a wide range of government projects. My role was to essentially play devil's advocate by identifying and mitigating the worst-case scenario. I was good at it, but after a while, I found myself doing this for everything. It was a rather pessimistic way of looking at the world, and in this pessimistic head-space, I knew that the job had lost its glow.

Every morning I'd cringe when the alarm went off (certainly no *carpe diem* here), drag myself out of bed, and begin the same morning ritual I've had for nearly ten years. This consisted of putting makeup on, drinking two cups of coffee to get the ole blood pumping, and then dashing out the door to brave the morning peak-hour traffic on the way to an office that seemed to be perpetually bathed in sickly green fluorescent lighting and buzzing with the incessant ringing of desk and mobile phones.

Trudging like the walking wounded through the jungle of cubicles to my desk every morning was tinged with the realisation that in a few minutes, after my computer had warmed up, I would be bombarded with a lengthy list of bold black emails in my inbox—some with their red "urgent" flags in the subject line visibly screaming their requests at me ASAP. The weekends would provide indispensable respite, but every Sunday night as

ANGELA LEMANIS

I set up the ironing board to iron my clothes for the approaching week, I would go into a depressive state just thinking that my weekend was over. I'd have to front up to work for five straight days before I could enjoy two precious days off again.

Believe me, that's no way to live—wishing away five days for the sake of two. I had to find something that I was passionate about and turn that into a living. But what the hell was I good at, that I really enjoyed, and could be turned into a lifestyle-sustaining career? Ah, that's the million-dollar question, my friend!

My father used to say to me when I was younger that if I had a difficult problem that needed an answer, I should take myself somewhere peaceful and spend quality thinking time mulling over the issue. I have done this in the past with other situations, and it always makes me feel better. The answers have always come, but probably because I gave them space to.

My dad first gave me this advice when I was twenty. I was struggling with questions about a new career path, and he told me to go outside into the garden and think about it in my own space. He said, "The answer might not come to you today, but if you continue to look at the situation in front of you, the answer will eventually materialise." So there I was late one afternoon, sitting in the back corner of my parent's garden on the old brick barbecue, weighing up the pros and cons of my problem. Quietly lying at my feet was Towser.

I looked at him and thought about all of the change he had been through in his life—leaving his mother, brothers, and sisters to go and live with four strangers; adapting to the comings and goings of our family's routine as we went to school, work, and sport; dealing with the absence of my brother Damian and I as we grew up and left home to start our adult lives; and moving from his first house in Sydney to his new home in Townsville when my parents decided that the tropical environment of North Queensland was the place to be. It occurred to me that he freely accepted these changes because he didn't have the fear of the unknown to distract him. He just went with the flow.

When I was fourteen years old, my family decided to spend our summer holidays in Townsville with my grandparents, and Towser came with us. To get from Sydney to Townsville involved two flights—one from Sydney to Brisbane, and one from Brisbane to Townsville. Towser had never flown before, so this was a big day for him. We had taken him to the vet beforehand who suggested that we tranquilise Towser to remove any potential anxiety that the flights might cause him. Poor Towser didn't have any warning of what was to come.

That morning—the first day of our holiday— Mum hid the tranquiliser tablet in his food and placed his stainless steel food bowl on the ground in front of him. She needn't have bothered hiding the tablet because everything in his bowl was always polished off within minutes of being served. When the family was ready to go, Towser was given one last chance to visit the backyard for a toilet stop before being placed in the car for the journey to the airport. At the airport, we stopped at the designated area where pets were to be dropped off for air travel. Towser's information was taken and he was weighed and sized up for his travel cage. By this time, the tranquiliser was starting to take effect and he appeared serene and sleepy, and completely unruffled by what was going on around him. It seemed a good time to take our leave. While Towser settled in to rest we parked the car and checked in for the first flight to Brisbane.

Arriving in Brisbane, I remember standing in the airport departure lounge waiting to board the second flight and looking out through the floor-to-ceiling windows at the plane on the tarmac. The ground crew were busy loading baggage and there, on a special trolley, was Towser waiting to be put on the plane. One of the ground crew was talking to him and patting him through the cage. The tranquiliser must have worn off a bit because Towser was reciprocating by vigorously wagging his tail and licking the crew member's hand. Instead of being wary or fearful of his new surroundings, Towser was taking it all in his stride—loud engine noise, the smell of jet fuel, strangers talking to him, and baggage and catering trucks passing by. He embraced all of the newness with a wag of his tail. I was so proud of him.

Three hours later we arrived in sunny Townsville. By the time we had retrieved our bags and hired the rental car, Towser was ready for collection. He had been released from his cage and was being given a quick walk around the hanger to stretch his legs when we pulled up. Upon seeing the family, he gave a couple of greeting barks and jerked his leash in our direction. Dad thanked the staff member for looking after him and walked Towser to the rental car for the short trip to our grandparent's place. Over half a day spent travelling the nearly 2000 kilometres from Sydney to Townsville hadn't taken a toll on Towser. He arrived in Townsville with as much enthusiasm as he had started out with that morning in Sydney.

ANGELA LEMANIS

So in light of my working situation in Auckland, I had to take a leaf out of Towser's book. If I couldn't accept the change with positivity and enthusiasm like he did, I needed to trust my instincts and put some distance between myself and the problem. I eventually resigned from my role and took some much-needed time to refocus and reassess. I went to my favourite park and spent time sitting under a sturdy pine tree with Max as my companion. I ran through a list of questions in my mind: What did I really want to do? What was I good at? Would doing this make me feel happy and fulfilled?

Bit by bit, I answered those questions in complete honesty. Not what others expected me to do or wanted me to do, but what I really wanted. The answer was writing this book and working part-time for my father's business while I did it.

Obviously, I had the luxury of taking time off to figure out my future prospects, and I realise how lucky that is in this day and age (and economy). But even now when I find myself facing change or a period of uncertainty, I focus on the aspects of my life that I can control so that there is continuity and stability in some areas while other areas are changing. Identifying the things that I can control is both reassuring and empowering.

Marilyn Monroe once said that "everything happens for a reason. People change so that you can learn to let go, things go wrong so that you appreciate them when they're right, . . . and sometimes good things fall apart so better things can fall together." Looking back on that time with my previous organisation, I'm pleased how it all turned out. The situation, whilst scary and unwelcomed at the time, was probably the best thing for me. It forced me to address some fears, to take some chances, and to go with the flow. Rather than resisting change, I had to accept that change will always occur, and that it needn't be feared.

My boxers have always freely accepted change in their lives. They are always looking for something new and are always ready to give something new a try. They do like their routine, but they also seem to know that change in any routine is good.

Change is healthy when embraced in a positive way. It keeps moving us forward, learning new things, and growing as people—and after all, isn't that what we're all here for? Change always serves to teach us something if we pay attention. It makes life exciting. It allows us to have new experiences; and it makes us cross paths with people who will have a fundamental impact on our lives. If it wasn't for change, my dogs would never have entered my life, and I can't imagine what that would have been like now. Obviously, some changes are harder to accept, but even when the change is upsetting and unwanted, you will be surprised by the way it can bring out the best in others. People will want to help you and be there for you, and when you look back on that time and are able to accept the change, you will see that some nice lessons were learned too.

ANGELA LEMANIS

LESSON 3

Me, Myself, and I:
Sometimes It's Good to Be Alone

OVER THE YEARS, I've had a like/strongly dislike relationship with being alone. During the first four years of my married life, I got to know just how much time alone is helpful and how much is simply too much.

My husband Andrej is a professional basketball coach, and during the first four years of our marriage, he spent part of the year regularly tripping to Australia for "away" games with the basketball team he coached. During the off-season, he was the assistant coach for the Australian men's basketball team, the Boomers, which was preparing for the London 2012 Olympics. He would finish his regular Australian National Basketball League (ANBL) season, and a month later, he would head away to the Aussie representative team camps and overseas tours. As soon as he returned from these, he'd be straight back into the next season with his ANBL team, the New Zealand Breakers. One year, he returned from an overseas trip in time to drive home from the airport, drop off his Boomers bag, pick up his NZ Breakers bag, and then leave for a week. In the space of twenty minutes, I had said hello and good-bye again.

All of that resulted in a very hectic schedule for him and a lot of alone time for me. At first, I thought, *This is great, I get the best of both worlds*. I can spend time with him while he's here doing "couple things," and when he's away, I can do the other things I enjoy that I otherwise wouldn't subject him to, like watching romantic comedy "chick flicks" and reading in bed until late at night.

After a while though, I began to miss having him around. Those first four years, he missed every birthday and wedding anniversary because of his touring schedule. The first wedding anniversary we spent together was our fifth! It was worth it though—the dream of being an Olympian is such a worthy pursuit, and I was exceptionally proud that he would have that experience. But meanwhile, it meant that I was a 'basketball widow' who would have to look at the schedule we kept on the fridge to know which country he was in at any given time. He was in so many of them: Spain, England, Argentina, Brazil, Turkey, Australia, China—and the list went on. I, of course, thought that his trips away with the team sounded glamorous, but I knew they were a lot of hard work. So even though he was visiting all of these foreign and picturesque countries, there was very little sight-seeing as he spent most of his time either in the hotel, in stadiums, or on the way to and from the hotel and stadium.

While he was away with the team, I'd find myself bumbling around the house, trying to find things to keep me entertained and to fill the sense of emptiness that had settled over the place. I was lonely and missed his company immensely. I knew I had struck a low point when I found myself in the midst of a Bridget Jones "All by myse-e-elf" moment one Friday night, sitting on the couch in my PJs, glass of red wine in hand, watching the tear-jerking, tug-on-your-heartstrings movie, *The Notebook*, and bawling my eyes out. I couldn't understand the sudden wave of emotion that had crashed over me. I had to pull myself together and get a grip. I could do this. I had lived alone before when I was single and had never had a problem with my own company. I reasoned with myself that I'd just forgotten how to be alone. But this time when Andrej was away, I had settled into a funk that was difficult to shift. It was like my coping mechanism had packed a bag, grabbed its passport, and left with my husband on a jet plane.

I couldn't even distract myself with domestic chores as there weren't as many to do when he was away. I didn't have the motivation to cook a meal for one every night, so I existed on toast and microwave meals for a while. One night, over a microwave macaroni and cheese, it dawned on me that my problem this time wasn't with being alone, it was being lonely—and there's a big distinction between the two. Loneliness, in my case, was not solely the absence of affection but the absence of direction. I needed a new focus in my life.

When Andrej did have one of his stints at home, we spoke about getting a boxer puppy. We had wanted one since we got married, but at the time, we were living in an apartment in the city. About six months after the wedding, we bought a house in a lovely, leafy green suburb in Auckland called Devonport. Close to the water, the village of Devonport is speckled with quaint heritage villas and bungalows and surrounded by numerous parks and walking areas, perfect for a dog. The time and place

ANGELA LEMANIS

seemed right to add a puppy to our family unit, and given my recent bout of loneliness, a dog would be a good companion to keep me company. Max was that puppy.

For the first six weeks that I had Max, Andrej was on the road. I used to hold Max up to the camera in our computer so that I could "Skype" Andrej and show him what our new puppy looked like. Max and I really bonded during that time because it essentially was just him and me (after Mum had gone back to Australia).

When Andrej did return home, Max was incredibly excited because here was another person who was going to shower him with cuddles and pats. They quickly became fast friends, which was evident one night when I came home from my regular evening jog to find Andrej asleep on the couch with Max curled up asleep on his chest, snoring.

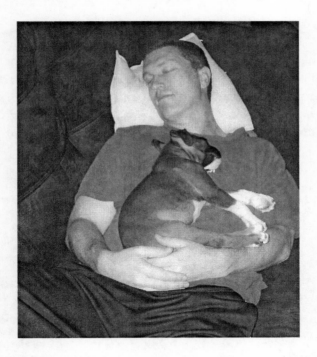

Max was great company. He added a vibrant energy to the house and kept me moving. We spent a lot of time outdoors, either walking or playing in the park or backyard. Each day, when I came home from work, he was there standing at the back door, excited to see me, tail wagging and bum wiggling. His front paws would be stomping at the ground as if the sheer joyfulness inside was proving difficult to contain. This exaggeratedly merry reception came to be known as his jelly bean dance. He'd wiggle his butt so much from side to side that his entire body resembled the shape of a jelly bean. His head would be cocked to the side, tongue hanging out, head bobbing up and down—it really was quite the sight. Sometimes I would also be greeted with a chorus of Chewbacca-inspired *woo woo woos* as if Max was trying to say hello. I'm convinced that everyone should be greeted by such excitement and love when they come home. Max wasn't upset that I'd left him, and he didn't seem to care where I'd been; he was just pleased that I came back. I could have had the crappiest day ever, but seeing such happiness upon returning home made even the worst troubles melt away instantaneously.

Having Max for company made such a difference. By nature, boxers love companionship. They are very loyal to their owners, but they're also independent and not at all needy. It was Max who showed me that being alone doesn't have to mean being lonely.

Max is a social creature who loves to be around Andrej and me and will most often be in the same room with us whenever we are home. But he also carves out alone time for himself during the day as well. He will soak up the sunshine in the backyard by himself for hours on end, and every night, he sits on the back deck. He is totally content during these times alone. He's doing exactly what he wants and is enjoying his own company.

Thinking back, Sammie also loved taking himself off on his own for some "mischief time." When he was two years old, he and I moved to a rural property in northern New South Wales, Australia. It was an area of high rainfall and acres of rolling hills and green pastures, perfect for dairy farming. It came as no surprise then that our property was surrounded on three sides by dairy farms. The cows resided up on the property that backed on to ours and also roamed on the hillsides to the left and right of our property. At the front, the land sloped gently down towards a dam on the forward boundary. The cows were nice neighbours who spent the majority of their time leisurely chewing on the grass and moving slowing from luscious green spot to luscious green spot. Sammie and I had moved there from North Queensland, the far north of Australia in the sunny tropics, so it was quite a change to be in the cooler, rainier southern part of the country.

The fences of the property were much farther away than the ones of the residential house where Sammie had grown up. With so much room to move around, he didn't quite know where to begin. At first, he stayed close to the house, but before long, his adventurous streak had him wandering farther away investigating every tree and wood heap in a one-kilometre radius. At first, I spent every moment watching him, like an overprotective mother, to make sure he didn't get into any trouble. There were no roads close by, so I wasn't concerned about that; but I did have worries that his curious nature would lead him astray, and he would inadvertently stumble across a poisonous snake or spider and try to "play" with it. The dam at the bottom of the property was also a source of apprehension for me because Sammie had never been around a large body of water before, and I wasn't sure if he would instinctively know how to swim. Ignoring my unease, he would often take off in a mad dash towards the dam only to stop just shy of the water. He would sniff at the plants around the edge of the dam and lean forward towards the water, but he never made the move to jump in. Seeing this behaviour, I felt better about letting him go down there.

One morning, I woke up to find that he wasn't in his usual spot on the porch. I assumed he was down at the dam so I headed off to see if I could find him. As I approached, I scanned the dam's edge to see if Sammie was in amongst the plants, but he was nowhere in sight. When I got a little closer, I saw ripples on the surface of the water and then a little black and white nose broke the water from underneath followed by half of his head. He saw me and the other ear momentarily came up out of the water before disappearing beneath again. It was clear that this swimming thing was not his forte! I called him to come towards me, and he started paddling with purpose but due to his dodgy dog paddle technique, instead of coming towards me in a straight line, he veered off to the left in an inadvertent semicircle. One leg was obviously paddling harder than the other, but he didn't seem overly concerned by this, except for the head shake he gave every few strokes to remove the water from his submerged left ear. Eventually, his series of long, slow arcs got him to the dam's edge where his paws could reach the shallower bottom. With great pride in himself, he bounced out of the water and onto dry land. Several fur shakes later—the likes of which would put my washing machine's spin cycle to shame—he was off again running up to the back of the property to find what else he could investigate.

One other morning, I caught him up visiting with the cows in the back paddock. One of the cows, Daisy, was licking him on the top of his head; and he stood there, nose in the air, enjoying every minute of it. Daisy was the only cow in the paddock that didn't have a calf. She had given birth, but her calf had died not long after. The other cows and calves kept their distance from her, but not Sammie. This particular morning was the first time I'd actually caught him in the paddock with her. He'd come back from there on a few previous occasions, fur all matted and stuck together with dried cow saliva, but I'd never actually seen them together. He stayed with Daisy by the fence line for about ten minutes—long enough to get a good dose of saliva from her and to give her face a few slobbery licks as well—before heading back down on to our property for a nap. He made this part of his daily ritual for the rest of the season before the cows were moved to a different paddock. Sammie was independent, but he always seemed to be around at the right time, and I'm sure his daily visits to keep Daisy company were more for her benefit than his. The next calving season, Daisy was seen in the paddock with a new calf of her own to care for, and Sammie never went to the back paddock again.

After seeing how content Max and Sammie were either in someone's company or completely by themselves, I saw that having time to spend alone is a positive thing if you spend the time well. I now look forward to finding new ways to spend my alone time, whether it be in the garden with a cup of coffee on a sunny morning, sitting on a bench at the beach reading a book, going for a long run with a medley of my favourite rock songs on my iPod, or "people-watching" over breakfast in a cosy Devonport cafe. Once I would never have gone to a cafe by myself because I'd be too worried that others would look at me with a pitiful look, as if I'd been stood up or I had no friends. Now I can sit in a cafe by myself, watching the world go by and feel completely at ease. During my "me time," I'm not accountable or responsible for anything other than enjoyment.

Being alone helps to recharge the battery. In this day and age, external distractions such as the phone and the computer compel us to stay connected with others; but time spent alone reconnects you to your body and spirit—the parts of you that aren't concerned with schedules, deadlines, or "have to do's." The beauty of time alone is that you have no one to talk to, but that's when you hear your thoughts and have an internal dialogue with yourself.

I appreciate being on my own now because I know that I'm not lonely. I have a husband that spends time away, but I know that he comes back too. I have a dog that is just as happy playing and walking with me as he is lying in the backyard by himself. At thirty-nine years of age, I've finally made my peace with being alone.

LESSON 4

Sleep = Sanity

O K, I HEAR you saying, "Really? That's a life lesson?" Well, yes, because it's taken me a while to realise just how important it is. The wonderful beings that helped me realise this important life lesson? My boxer dogs, of course—the gurus of sleep themselves. Their pure dedication to sleep has elevated it to an art form in my house. After plenty of trial and error, I am convinced that sleep equals sanity—it's a simplistic equation, but unfortunately not many of us get it, enough sleep that is.

Epic rock band Bon Jovi provided us with the catchy lyrical phrase:

> Until I'm six feet under,
> Baby, I don't need a bed,
> Gonna live while I'm alive,
> I'll sleep when I'm dead.

Good for you, Mr. Bon Jovi, but I'll take my sleep every night, eight straight solid hours of it, thank you very much. If you save sleep for when you're dead, then you just found a sure-fire way to fast-track that process!

According to the World Association of Sleep Medicine, sleeplessness is a global epidemic that threatens mental, physical and emotional health, and quality of life. When you are sleep deprived, you're more susceptible to colds, flu, other viruses and infections; may experience depression, anxiety, irritability, and mood swings; can forget important information and display poor judgement and poor concentration; can have a reduced ability to deal with stress; and could increase your risk of obesity, heart disease, and diabetes. And these are just a few of the side effects. No wonder sleep deprivation has been used throughout history as a torture technique!

The body repairs itself during sleep, so logic suggests that getting enough of the right kind of sleep is beneficial to overall health and well-being. At least eight hours of sleep can reduce stress and inflammation in the body and repair the damage received during the day from ultraviolet rays and other harmful environmental exposures.

In my teen years and in my twenties, I could sleep like a champion. I'd easily get my eight hours a night, and on the weekend, I could sleep for fourteen hours a night—finally surfacing at 11:00 am. In my thirties, things changed. I began to have nights where I would either have trouble falling asleep or I would wake in the wee small hours of the morning and then have trouble getting back to sleep. The common cause of my sleeplessness? Worry.

I am a second-generation worrywart. My mum has always been a worrier, and hence a bad sleeper because she lies awake at night worrying about my brother and me or work or anything that is proving concerning to her at the time. And as if by flicking a switch, I seemed to inherit this nasty little habit in my thirties. I would keep myself awake at night, worrying about something/anything while my husband was sound asleep beside me.

Sometimes I would begin worrying the moment my head hit the pillow because for the first time that day, everything was quiet, and I had time to think. At other times, I would fall asleep quickly but then wake up just after two in the morning and worry about what I had to do the next day. The mental checklist would come out, and I'd run through it item by item instead of trying to go back to sleep. Soon worrying about the things I had to do the next day was replaced with anxiety over the sleep I was currently losing, and I'd fret that I'd be tired the next day, which would make everything worse. Follow this with frustration and anger at my lack of sleep and by 4:00 am, I had run the gauntlet of emotions, and the sun hadn't even come up yet. What a way to start the day!

Author F. Scott Fitzgerald once said that, "The worst thing in the world is to try to sleep and not to." Stress and worry can be the biggest factors in preventing a good night's sleep. Worrying keeps the mind stimulated, which makes it harder to fall asleep and also causes the hormone adrenaline to be released which works against the body's ability to doze off.

In my moments of worry-induced sleeplessness, I'd often look at Max sleeping (and most often snoring) on his beanbag with not a care in the world. None of my boxers ever looked like they were dealing with life's problems in the middle of the night. Not that I would ever really know, but from the snoring, rapid eye movement, and leg twitches that consistently occurred, it seemed like they all enjoyed regular deep sleep.

ANGELA LEMANIS

When Max was little, he slept on a large European pillow. As a puppy, he'd sleep on his side with his back paws up around his mouth. His sleep appeared restful, except for the puppy dreams he'd have where he would emit high-pitched barks for about thirty seconds before sleeping quietly again. Even now, as a three-year-old, he sleeps in this same position when it's "serious sleep time," and his "dream barks" remain at the same high-pitched tone as they were when he was little.

As Max got older and larger, we gave him a beanbag as his dog bed. He loved it because he could push it around with his nose and his front paws in order to make it just right for sleeping. Every night at 7:00 pm, my husband and I watch as Max goes to his beanbag and turns around and around in circles, pushing at the beanbag until he gets it in the perfect position. Then he collapses down onto it, lets out a big sigh, and goes to sleep.

Every now and then though, he struggles to get his beanbag right. One such night, I was sitting on the couch, and he was circling 'round and 'round more times than usual. He'd stop, push the beanbag with his nose a few times, and repeat the circling again. After about two minutes of this, he came over to where I was sitting, plopped his head on my knee, and looked up at me with tired, bloodshot eyes as if to say, "It's not working. Please help me." I went over and moved the beanbag around for him so that the centre was slightly dipped. He climbed in, laid his head on the raised edge, and promptly fell asleep.

Sammie was also a true sleep aficionado. He could fall asleep easily in any situation and under any conditions, be it in the beanbag, on the floor, out in the yard, on the couch, or in my bed. The problem for Sammie was that he had a rather pronounced under bite and a tongue that seemed far too long for his mouth. I noticed this when I got him as a puppy—it didn't matter how far away I thought my face was from his, his long tongue would unfurl quickly like that of a frog's, and I'd end up with a slobbery lick across the face.

When Sammie slept, the tip of his tongue would often hang out by about two inches and move up and down as he breathed in and exhaled. Having a bit of fun one morning, I slunk down onto the ground beside where he was sleeping deeply and gently grabbed the tip of his exposed tongue and pulled it out slowly so that it was extended almost as far as it would go. Sammie didn't stir once as I did this, even though I was trying my best to stifle a giggle. He lay there, sleeping and snoring with his tongue

ANGELA LEMANIS

protruding on the floor in front of him for close to half an hour. Eventually he woke and, noticing that his tongue had dried out like an old sponge, spent the next few minutes licking continually in order to moisten it before resuming his sleep again.

Dogs enjoy sleep because I'm convinced that on some ancient predatory level, they know how important it is for their survival. Dogs also sleep well because they aren't affected by the typical culprits of sleeplessness such as worry, stress, and anxiety.

Worrying is a habit just like any other habit. The future can't be predicted. Setting goals and making practical plans is responsible, but the rest can't be controlled. The only moment that can be influenced by us is the present one. Worrying serves no purpose at all—it is only an illusion of control, and there's no point in losing sleep over an illusion. Just like the proverb, "Let sleeping dogs lie," I have learnt to leave my problems alone at night and not go messing with them.

Now if I have a problem that is proving difficult to fix or is worrying me, I sleep on it. I imagine the problem written down on a piece of paper and then, I mentally fold the paper up into a tiny package and put it in a box. I say to myself, "OK, subconscious, over to you. You're in charge of this while I sleep." I put the problem out of my mind, knowing that my deeper subconscious is working through the problem for me while I get a good night's sleep. I always wake up refreshed and with a much better perspective in the morning. If the problem is still there, I will think about it a few times during the day and then repeat the process that night of putting it away in a box. After a couple of days, I either have an answer to the problem or it disappears off my radar completely.

After watching Max and how easily he can fall asleep, I figured that it's not just the lack of worry that helps him; it's also because he tends to sleep at regular times. He wakes up at the same time each day (you could set your clock by him), he doesn't watch television until late at night, he eats the same size meal at the same time every night, and he doesn't have caffeine or alcohol in his system. But the big thing is that he seems to listen to his own body. When Max is tired at night, he sleeps. He doesn't fight it like I've been known to do some nights when I'm sitting up to watch my favourite TV show when I really should be listening to my body and heading off to bed.

Now I make a ritual of going to bed. I begin with a relaxing hot shower. Mum used to say to me when I was younger that having a shower at night washes away all the cares of the day. This resonated with me (yes, Mum, I did listen to you some of the time), and to this day, I still imagine all of the daily worries being washed down the drain with the shower water. I continue to wind myself down by doing some light reading before calling it a night. Bed is now my "happy place" (along with Disneyland, but that's another story) because I know wholeheartedly that sleep is the best medicine for all that ails you.

Sleep equals sanity because it helps to maintain your balance and perspective. When I didn't sleep well, the beginning of each day felt like the end of the world. Now that I've learned the importance of being well-rested, my days start out on a cheerier note—normally with Max pawing at the doona cover at my feet encouraging me to get up. When I raise my head to look at him, I get to see the first wiggle of his tail for the day, and I'm ready to go out and face the world.

Know What You Want:
Sorting the Peas from the Gravy

K NOWING WHAT YOU want is only part of the equation. The rest of it consists of knowing what you will accept, what you will change, and what you will walk away from. Knowing what you want is more powerful than knowing what you don't want because it comes from a place of positivity as opposed to a place of fear and negativity. We can all immediately conjure up thoughts of what we don't want—we don't want to be poor, sick, unhappy, stressed, and so on. But knowing what you truly want in life is trickier—it requires reflection and a good understanding of who you are. This comes with time, experience, and learning from our mistakes.

My boxers have always been very straightforward when it came to knowing what they did or didn't want. As any boxer dog owner will tell you, they are an intelligent and energetic breed, but they can also be incredibly stubborn and headstrong too. One needs a lot of patience to be the owner of a boxer, and believe me, they will test it regularly. Towser, Sammie, and Max all pushed the boundaries and, in doing so, quickly figured out what they liked and disliked.

Almost from the second month we had Towser, we noticed that he didn't like to go outside to sleep at night. The first month he was with us, Towser slept inside in a box because he was so little but when he was thirteen weeks old, my parents insisted that he sleep outside on the back veranda in his purpose-built kennel. The kennel was a large well-built wooden structure that had several blankets inside for him to snuggle into and keep warm. Towser, however, didn't like being relegated outside and separated from us each night. His cunning plan to get around being put out? He burrowed in behind the couch cushions so that he was mostly hidden from view. The first time he did this, Mum was temporarily hoodwinked. She searched for him in the family room and not finding him, she thought he might already have been put outside. She checked outside and couldn't find him there either. Walking back into the family room, she noticed the cushions moving and a little boxer butt jutting out from behind one of them. Mum snatched up the cushions and there he was, all curled up, trying his best to be invisible. He was promptly sent outside much to his disappointment. In the parents-versus-puppy contest, the score was Parents: 1, Towser: zip. Maybe the path of least resistance for my parents would have been to leave Towser inside as much as possible given the stunt he was about to pull next.

Our family home was a gorgeous three-level structure that tiered its way down a slight hillside in our Sydney suburb. The top floor was at street level and housed the bedrooms, bathroom, laundry, and entrance hall. The second floor contained the formal living and dining areas and the kitchen, and the lower level consisted of the family room which led out to a veranda and gardens.

Down one side of the house, my parents had a beautiful split-level Japanese-style garden complete with volcanic rocks and sedimentary stones, water feature, and a pond with several goldfish. The bottom of the garden led into a paved barbecue area and a long, narrow section of grass. It was a fantastic place to raise a family and a spacious outdoor area for Towser to run around in. Despite my parents' initial misgivings, Towser didn't show any interest in the garden or the goldfish pond. Towser was happiest spending time inside with us whenever we were home. If we weren't, he'd laze in the sun on the paved bricks or run around on the grassed section.

One spring Saturday afternoon, my parents decided to add a few plants to the garden. After spending a small fortune at the local plant nursery on some calla lilies with beautiful orange flowers, they headed home to plant them. Towser was enthralled by the activity and carefully watched Mum and Dad from his sunny spot on the pavers as they dug holes, upended plants from their pots, and buried them into the rich, dark soil. When all was done, they cleaned up and headed inside with Towser in tow.

Monday rolled around—my parents left for work, and my brother and I made tracks to school. Before leaving, we gave Towser a pat and sent him outside for the day. I was the first to return home that afternoon, and after kicking off my school shoes and dropping my backpack on the bedroom floor, I raced down to the family room to see Towser standing on the other side of the glass sliding door waiting to come in. His stumpy tail was wagging vigorously, but something was different about his body language. His head was hanging low, and his eyes peered up at me. I'd only ever seen this look when he was apologising for something—it was his "I'm sorry" look.

"What have you done, mister?" I asked in a low tone, to which he lowered his head even farther and looked away. His tail was still wagging but a little more unsurely than before. It was then that I thought of the garden.

"Oh, you're going to be in so much trouble," I said as I headed down the back steps.

Towser, who would normally be right by my side whenever I was in the backyard, stayed in his spot by the back door. Turning around to look up at the split-level garden, I saw his destructive handiwork. Every calla lily that my parents had lovingly planted on Saturday afternoon was ripped out and discarded, leaving several ugly dark ruptures in the landscape of the otherwise colourful (and untouched) garden. I called his name, and his little head peeked around the top of the steps.

"Come here," I said, and he reluctantly did the walk of shame down the back steps and over to where I was standing. Pointing to the garden, I said, "What did you do?" He looked in the direction of my pointed finger and then at me, as if to say, "Wonder how that happened?" The look in his eyes may have feigned innocence, but his body language betrayed him. He couldn't have looked guiltier than if the word was spray-painted in red across his fur. I did my best to minimise the damage by clearing the discarded plants before my parents came home, but there was no doubt, my parents were not going to be pleased.

We didn't have long to wait before Mum arrived home. I told her what had happened, and she was cranky but also knew that not much could be done about it at that point. Dad was more upset—especially at the waste of time and money—but he too knew there was no point in closing the proverbial stable door after the horse had bolted. What was done was done. Dad was now focused on making sure it didn't happen again.

His plan to outwit Towser's newfound repugnance of orange calla lilies involved the weekend, some timber posts, and an electric fence. A colleague of Dad's had a portable low-voltage electric fence that could be easily erected as a barrier for a small area. Dad explained the situation and asked if he could borrow the fence for a month, to which his colleague obliged. That following weekend, Mum and Dad returned to the plant nursery, purchased more calla lilies, and planted them in the holes where the previous lilies had been. Towser watched with interest as they went about their work, probably confused as to why they were doing this strange ritual again. After planting and cleaning the area up, I helped Dad unfurl the electric fence and secure it so that all sides of the garden were covered. He switched it on and tested it with the back of his hand to check the voltage level. The barrier gave a slight sting when touched, but nothing more than that. "Right, let's see if that deters you" he said to Towser before they both headed up the back steps and inside.

Monday was the test, the first time Towser had been left alone outside all day. Mum and Dad were pleasantly surprised that afternoon to see that everything in the garden was as it should be—in place and intact. Dad went down to have a closer look and noticed that Towser kept a healthy distance from the fence.

"Did it get you?" he questioned Towser as he went closer to the fence. "You'll be fine if you just stay away from it."

Towser's look seemed to agree—once bitten, twice shy!

After two weeks of having the fence switched on and the garden completely untouched, Dad decided to turn the voltage off. The fence would remain as a physical barrier; it just wouldn't provide a shock. Given that Towser was keeping his distance from it, we figured that he wouldn't even know that it had been switched off. Another week passed and everything was fine. The new plants were bedding in nicely, so nicely that Dad purchased a few more and planted them. Four days later, Mum came home from work to find Towser at the back door, tail wagging, waiting to come in. Bending down to give him a pat, she noticed the tell-tale evidence that suggested a crime had occurred. Towser's front paws were muddy. She raced past him to the back steps, and there in front of her lay a vision of wilful destruction. One side of the electric fence was lying flat on the ground, and every single plant that had been added over the past three weeks was uprooted and tossed aside. The original plants were untouched—it was only the new ones that Towser (the garden anarchist) had taken issue with. Towser must have brushed past the fence at some point during the day, realised he didn't get a shock from it, and then got on with his landscaping job. Needless to say, Dad was not a happy chappy when he returned home that night and saw the results of Towser's garden romp, but that was the end of the electric fence (it went back to Dad's work colleague the next day), and it was the last time my parents tried to add plants to the Japanese gardens. Towser: 1, parents: 1—the start of many battles of the wills over the years.

Sammie also knew with certainty what he wanted. He wanted to get towel dried after his baths; he wanted to run around the backyard in circles every afternoon at 5:00 pm just because it felt good; he wanted to swing off the clothes on the clothesline; and he wanted to eat leftover stew over his normal dog food any day. He always sorted the peas from the gravy though. Sammie didn't like peas, and even though the stew had the peas and other vegetables incorporated with the gravy and the meat, I would come back to find a spotlessly clean and shiny bowl with all of the green peas sitting in the bottom of it. Each pea had been completely licked clean of any gravy remnants and was still in one piece. I guess he just didn't like peas.

As for the clothes, I had no knowledge of his naughty little escapades until a neighbour approached me in the driveway when I arrived home one afternoon.

"Excuse me," she said, "do you know that your dog swings from your clothes when they're on the clothesline?"

"Uh . . . no, I wasn't aware of that."

"Yes, I've watched him. He holds on by his mouth and swings back and forth," the neighbour informed me.

No wonder I had teeth marks on the bottom of my good trousers! I thanked her for letting me know.

One morning, soon after my neighbour's exposé of my dog's secret clothesline antics, I hung some sheets out, said good-bye to Sammie, and then pretended to leave. The stakeout had begun. I spied on him as he disappeared around the back of the house where the clothesline was and then snuck back into the yard without him knowing. I watched as Sammie sniffed at the sheets and then wandered a few metres away from the clothesline before turning, taking a run up, and launching himself off the ground. He grabbed the corner of one of the bed sheets with his mouth and held on tightly. His eyes were closed and his legs hung limply as his little body swung back and forth like a pendulum on a grandfather clock.

Wanting to catch him in action, I acted fast. I did the stealthiest tiptoe I knew. I got within one metre of the back of him undetected before saying in my most authoritative voice, "And what do you think you're doing?"

His body jumped in startled surprise; he had no idea I'd crept up behind him. His eyes darted over in my direction while he simultaneously let go of the sheet. He knew he was sprung but tried to appease me with a wag of his tail.

"I don't think so, buddy, you're not going to waggle your way out of this one."

Pointing to the sheet, I said, "No," and touched the bottom corner of it for added emphasis. He sat down apologetically and stayed there while I pegged the bottom of the sheets up so that he couldn't get at them again. And he didn't—after being caught in the act, his swinging days were over.

Max had his own ideas about what he wanted too. One afternoon, I was driving home from work. It had been a good day—a serious deadline that had been looming was met, and I was looking forward to going home and relaxing on the couch with a glass of wine. Walking into the kitchen towards the French doors that lead to the backyard, I noticed something odd through the kitchen windows. Instead of a small paved area followed by a mass of green lawn, the entire area was a whiteout as if dusted in a fine layer of snow. This of course was not possible in autumn in Auckland. Opening the French doors and stepping outside, I was greeted by a very excitable Max with some of the "snow" in his mouth. I reached in and wiped it out from his jowls and noticed that the snowlike substance was in fact white polystyrene beanbag beans. The yard was covered in thousands of them! Sitting in the centre of the white coverage was the remains of the beanbag cover.

Max had obviously taken a dislike to the new supersized outdoor beanbag that my husband and I had bought him the day before for the inside of his kennel. The kennel, being quite large, had a wooden floor which could get cold in winter so we got a flat, rectangular beanbag to provide cushioning for him to lie on whenever we went out. For whatever reason, Max didn't want it in his kennel and had spent the day wrestling it out through the kennel's doorway and ripping it to shreds. My lovely vision of relaxing on the couch went completely out the window. Instead, I spent the next hour vacuuming the backyard—much to the amusement of my neighbours. Who knew polystyrene beans were so hard to get rid of! They stuck together with static cling, which the vacuum cleaner only exacerbated, and the afternoon breeze didn't help either. My poor Dyson vacuum cleaner with its super-duper trademarked Cyclone technology meant that it had plenty of suction but not much room in the collection chamber for this type of job. I must have emptied it a hundred times before most of the beans were collected. Max, who had been relegated inside to stop him from pouncing at the beans and dispersing them further, was watching through the doors while I finished vacuuming the backyard. My attention was focused on the lookout for any large polystyrene-covered mounds knowing what potentially might lie underneath.

ANGELA LEMANIS

In all of his doggie wisdom, Max knew what he wanted and didn't want—he wanted to play with the beanbag, and he didn't want it in his kennel. So, in all of my human wisdom, I complied with his wishes—he never got an outdoor beanbag for his kennel again.

As easy as it was for my dogs to know what they wanted and didn't want, it was harder for me to reconcile. Knowing what you want means knowing how (and when) to say *no*. Knowing it and voicing it are two different things. It has taken me many years to begin feeling okay about saying no to someone. There have been so many occasions where I've been invited to large functions either for work or socially. I don't like going to large functions because crowds make me uncomfortable, as does the small talk that usually occurs when you put a lot of people together. So many times I've really wanted to say *no* and not go, but I couldn't find a way to decline without feeling bad about it. In the end, I'd go to the function only to wind up feeling ashamed at myself for not having had the courage and gumption to decline. This has been a recurring theme throughout my life. I say *yes* when I feel pressured—even by persistent salespeople—because I don't want to disappoint or let people down, and I don't like confrontation. Saying *yes* is the path of least resistance, but it always left me feeling mad at myself. I resented my inability to say *no* and my lack of living in authenticity. I felt like other people were controlling my life and I was cowardly going along for the ride rather than asserting myself. I even had difficulty saying *no* to myself.

Knowing what you want doesn't always mean it's good for you. Sometimes you just have to be realistic about what you can actually do. In 2009, I decided that I was going to run a marathon in August followed by an ultramarathon in October. I had been regularly running for nine years, and I wanted to complete both without injury. For eight months, my spare time was consumed by a regimented training programme. At one stage, I was running ten hours (the equivalent of more than two marathons) every weekend, not to mention the long training runs I did during the week. All in all, I was clocking up over 150 kilometres each week. On top of all the training, my workload at work was increasing. I had also signed up to do a management course, which required me to study externally and complete an assignment each week. So I added this new activity to the training schedule, my full-time job, and all of the other mundane yet necessary weekly tasks that needed to be done (grocery shopping, laundry, cleaning, etc).

I completed the marathon, ultramarathon, and graduated from the management course; but the stress I had placed on my body and mind over the course of the year resulted in me getting sick—first with anaemia and then with shingles. The anaemia I could handle with a few iron injections and a change in my diet, but the shingles required an immediate cessation of work and exercise, and bed rest for over a month. It was painful too. What was more painful to deal with was that I had brought this on myself.

This was my body's last ditch attempt to make me pay attention and slow down. I had ignored the signs and signals my body had been giving me to slow down at my own peril. The body is funny like that—it will start out subtly and then when you continue to ignore its signs, it will take over and make you sit up and listen. When I thought back to how I managed to get myself into such a pickle, it came down to my inability to say *no* both at work and in my own personal life. It was an inability to understand my own limitations and to work within them. In my stubborn mind, I thought that I could just keep ploughing through and then when Christmas came and I got my annual holidays, I could rest knowing that I'd achieved everything I had set out to do that year. I was burning through adrenaline on a daily basis, supplementing the exhaustion with coffee, carbohydrates, and a steely-minded determination. But alas, I didn't even make it to the holidays that year—the brakes came on in November.

Looking back now, I was lucky that I only got shingles out of my exhaustion and stress. Others who are less fortunate find the mixture of exhaustion, stress, and burning the candle at both ends can lead to heart attacks, severe flu, or accidents. The human body is not supposed to operate at that capacity long-term, and mine forced me to stop and take some time out to recover. While that got me well again in the safety and security of my own house, it didn't address the problem that put me there. When I really analysed why I found it so difficult to say *no*, I found that it was because I wanted to please others. I didn't want to disappoint them or let them down. I didn't want them to think differently about me if I didn't do what they requested. I wanted to be the person they could rely on—the person who came through and got things done. It had to stop. As difficult or uncomfortable as it was for me to say *no*, I had to learn that it was my right to do so.

Saying *no* is just refusing a request, not rejecting the person. But it was how I went about saying *no* that I needed to master. Firstly I had to learn to say *no* with confidence and not get dragged into a negotiation with someone who wanted to press the point and turn my initial *no* into

ANGELA LEMANIS

an eventual *yes*. I also had to learn that it's best to give a concise "no, thank you" and leave it at that rather than blather on with a long-winded explanation as to why I was declining. I had to realise that my *no* on its own was good enough. I didn't owe anyone an explanation.

Saying *no* can be very liberating when you understand that it is just the answer to a question. Being true to yourself and your wishes is a choice like any other, and I would rather say a considered and meaningful *no* to something I don't want to do than give a half-hearted *yes* and regret the decision later. When you listen and comply with your real thoughts and feelings, saying *no* to something that doesn't appeal or feel right means that you're saying *yes* to yourself—yes that you heard your intuition and trusted it.

Dogs—well, all animals—do this as they are instinctual by nature. So are we, but too often that inner voice of reason gets drowned out by the external noise. Everything is a choice, and after many, many hit-and-miss attempts, I'm glad to say that for now I know what I want. I know what I can achieve; I know my limitations, and I know I can say *no* and be OK with it. After watching Sammie all those years ago sort his peas from the gravy, I can now metaphorically do the same.

LESSON 6

All That Glitters . . . Is Just Shiny

GREEK PHILOSOPHER AND all-round smart guy Socrates once said, "He is the richest who is content with the least." Unfortunately in today's modern society, it can be difficult to conduct one's life in accordance with this ethos as we are bombarded with the new "must-have" gadgets and widgets, or the latest cutting-edge technologies emerging onto the market.

As those who know me would attest, I have in the past been particularly partial to anything shiny and new. Even as a youngster, my parents affectionately called me Bowerbird because I would accumulate anything glittery, glossy, or brightly coloured.

As an adult, I graduated from being a Bowerbird (who merely collected the shiny things around me) to being a marketer's dream who actively sought out brand-new sparkly things—much to my husband's exasperation. All I needed to be given was one good reason why I should have this new thing, and I was hooked. "Yes," the little voice in my head says, "you do need that. And what's more, you didn't even know you needed it! How have you possibly survived without it until now?" My husband couldn't understand how quickly I went from having no prior knowledge of a product to deciding that I simply couldn't live without it. I must admit, there was no logic to my decisions whatsoever. My rose-coloured glasses came on, and I became mesmerised by the pretty new thing.

But . . . (here I go clutching at straws as I begin my futile attempt at defending my behaviour) it wasn't entirely my fault! Marketers target people like me by using psychologist Carl Rogers's concept of appealing to our "ideal self" as opposed to our "real self." Marketers show us how their product can improve our lives and potentially the way others perceive us, and how spending disposable income on their product can help us attain the so-called good life.

Of course, the logical side of me knows that I'm being marketed to, but the product is so shiny and new that I do think it would (a) make my life easier if I had it; (b) make me feel better about myself if I had it; (c) improve my image if I had it; or d) all of the above! Gimme, gimme, gimme, let the retail therapy begin! The "high" of the buy evaporates relatively quickly afterwards—especially if the gap between the purchase and the credit card statement is a short one—and even though I still like the purchase, it invariably never lives up to the marketing promise of improving my life, my self-image, or my public persona.

After being bombarded with messages from advertisers, telling us how we are somehow lacking if we don't have the latest mobile phone, designer jacket, or celebrity fragrance, it is easy to feel not good enough if we don't keep up with the latest fashions or trends. A friend of mine bought into this type of thinking that having pretty, expensive things would make her happier or more acceptable to others. She purchased an exorbitantly priced (but gorgeous) designer-label handbag, but it turned out to be more of a status symbol; a statement that she could afford a ridiculously overpriced handbag rather than just a bag to keep her wallet, phone, and sunglasses safe. Then I realised that everything she owned made a statement. There were the Dolce & Gabbana sunglasses, the iPhone, the Prada shoes—and the list went on. Granted, I thought her belongings were beautiful until I noticed that her individuality was being minimised by the brand statements she was layering herself with. People would talk to her, but the whole time, they were commenting on her new watch, her gorgeous shoes, her new jacket. No one seemed interested in her or how she was doing. Suddenly I wasn't so envious of the things she had. This poor girl was being drowned out by labels as if they were the only things of value. She was "branded."

The saddening thing is that she believed these products would make her feel better, but instead she was hiding behind them. It's a mistake to be defined in your own mind by what you have—people have much more to offer than their materialistic bottom line. But understanding the root cause of the need to smother ourselves in expensive items or craving the "high" of the buy means being present and seeing things for what they actually are, not what they might potentially represent. Take it from me. After years of trying, I've realised you just can't shop your way to happiness.

Mahatma Gandhi believed that materialism was the "central evil of the modern world." And while some might think this is a fairly harsh statement, materialism, conspicuous consumption, and "keeping up with the Joneses," coupled with easier access to credit, has resulted in an increase in addictive spending and mounting personal debt. We are living in a society where people feel pressure to live outside their means, and this leads to overspending on credit cards and the like. Despite the challenges a fragile economy presents for the average consumer, we are being marketed to at an ever-increasing rate by a relentless multibillion dollar marketing machine.

The cautionary tale here is that all that glitters is not gold . . . it's just shiny. Materialistic pursuits are not a pathway to happiness, regardless of what the marketing machine promises. Instead, the acquisition of "things" in order to feel this false happiness can make us slaves to our own desires and prisoners to our bills. The thing is that we have everything we need to be content now. Forget the "price tag society" we live in and the marketing that promises to rid us of our insecurities if we buy the products guaranteeing perfection, the items offering fulfilment, and the thingamajigs providing ease and comfort. Real value comes from our experiences, not from our purchases. It's the stuff that's not for sale that's the most important—the relationships with your family members, the relationship with yourself and your internal thoughts, the peace of mind that comes from feeling true happiness. We need to spend more time being grateful for the things that we have now rather than always wishing that it would be bigger, better, faster. More is just that—more.

My boxers have confirmed that you really don't need a lot to be happy. But even a dog can be swayed by the temptation of something new.

Right from puppyhood, Sammie kept his few worldly possessions in a pile near his dog bed. His pile consisted of one of my mum's old shoes, his ball, one red sock, and a stick. Despite dogs being colour blind, Sammie always coveted red-coloured items. If it was red, he was drawn to it. He treasured his few possessions and kept them together unless he was playing with one of them, in which case, he would always bring it back to his pile when he was finished with it.

When Sammie was just over a year old, I was studying and had set up a small home office so that I had a place to study and keep my textbooks, computer, and stationery supplies. Bit by bit, my stationery supplies started to mysteriously vanish. First, it was the glue stick, then the stapler. I thought I was going crazy as I could have sworn those items were there the day before they disappeared.

In the middle of doing housework one Saturday afternoon, I looked up from the vacuuming in time to see Sammie's rear end disappear around the corner of the hallway into the home office. Curious as to what he was doing, I quietly placed the still-running vacuum down and followed him, peering around the doorway of the office just in time to see him rear up on his hind legs and place his front paws on the top of the desk. With his mouth open and tilted to the side, he carefully grabbed hold of the sticky tape dispenser. Once securely in place between his jaws, he plopped back down onto all four feet again and wandered out of the office towards the front door while I hid down the hallway out of sight. When I thought it was safe, I followed him and saw him head outside and disappear around the corner of the house in the direction of the garden shed. I stepped outside and followed quietly. There, in between the back of the garden shed and the fence, I noticed he had already dug a hole, and he was in the process of dropping the sticky tape dispenser into it when I made my presence known.

Not knowing that I had followed him, he was incredibly surprised when I said, "What are you doing?" He responded with a startled twitch. Knowing that he was caught red-handed in the midst of his misdemeanour, he lowered his head and tentatively wandered towards me as I approached the freshly dug hole. Looking up at me, he gave a few apologetic wags of his tail as he looked from me to the hole and back again. There in the hole was my recently pilfered sticky tape dispenser alongside my previously stolen glue stick and stapler. The items in Sammie's stationery stockpile were still in one piece and in good condition with only a few teeth marks and some dirt attached. I couldn't understand why he was so attracted to these items until I realised they were all red in colour. Sammie seemed quite proud of his secret red stash but also knew he was probably going to get reprimanded for taking them. I couldn't help but smile though and had to feign sternness as I pointed to his stockpile and gently said *no*. I collected the items and saw his disappointment as he sat looking at the now-empty hole. After a quick clean, the stationery items were returned to the safety of my desk drawer.

The most prized possession for Towser, Sammie, and Max was their tennis ball—it was the only possession they really needed. Towser's ball was never far from his sight, and every time I ventured into the backyard—whether it was going to the clothesline or watering the plants—he saw it as an opportunity to play ball. The only problem with Towser's "game" was that he didn't understand the concept of bringing the ball back. I would walk to one end of the yard and throw the ball towards the other end. Towser would hare off towards the direction of the thrown ball and then stop where the ball had fallen onto the ground. He'd look up at me, back down at his ball, and up at me again waiting for me to make the first move. I'd wait for a few minutes to see if Towser was going to pick the ball up and bring it back to me; but after a while, he would lie down next to the ball, put his head on the ground, and stare at me. Knowing that he wasn't going to move, I'd walk to where he and the ball were and throw it to the opposite end of the yard. Off Towser would go in a mad rush, only to stop and sit where the ball had landed while I wandered up the yard to where he was. I guess we were both getting exercise, but I secretly envied those dog owners who could sit in an outdoor chair, cool drink in hand, throwing the ball for their dog who obediently brought it back and dropped it on their lap. This was not going to be my reality with Towser . . . or Sammie for that matter.

Sammie loved chasing his ball. As with Towser before him, the fetching component needed work—sometimes he would, most often he wouldn't. Most times, I would throw the ball and he'd chase it down, pick it up in his mouth, and then refuse to drop it. I'd try to get it out of his mouth and he'd run just out of reach. I knew the first few times this happened that Sammie saw this as a much better game because I would chase him. Once I stopped chasing him, he would drop the ball so that I could throw it again. While I know that Dog Whisperer Cesar Millan would shake his head at this (I can almost hear him saying that to be the pack leader, I should be controlling the game and setting rules, boundaries, and limitations for playtime—and he would be 100 percent right of course), I played this way with Sammie because he seemed to enjoy the interaction so much. I'd chase him 'round and 'round the backyard, and he would always scoot just out of my reach and swiftly change direction and go running right past me. Sometimes I anticipated his escape route, and he'd have to duck or back track so that I couldn't grab the ball out of his mouth but nine times out of ten; he was just too fast for me. It meant that Sammie rarely fetched the ball and brought it back to me, but I could live with that.

I was determined not to perpetuate that behaviour with Max though. I did want one of my boxers to be able to bring the ball back to me, and Max does. It took some work though. Max didn't understand what a ball was when he was a puppy. Mum bought him his first tennis ball, and he was curious at how it rolled around on the ground but didn't really understand what to do with it. He would watch it and then look at me for an explanation as to what I expected him to do with it. But it didn't take long for him to see how much fun it could be to chew on, and push around with his paws, and chase once it started to bounce off into the distance.

Max quickly discovered how to throw the ball around for himself—using his mouth to throw the ball and then chasing after it and pouncing on it, or bashing it around with his front paws like a football player does with his feet.

Max loves his ball so much that he likes to carry it in his mouth when we go for walks to the park. Once at the park, we play with it, but I have to carry it home because he's normally panting by then and finds it difficult to pant and have something in his mouth at the same time.

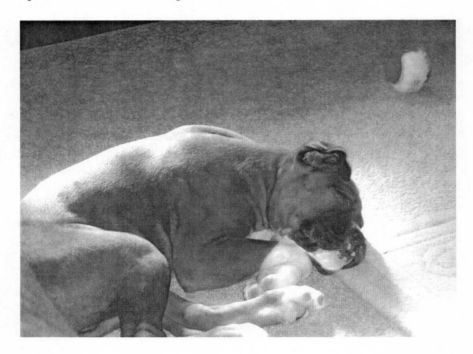

These treasured items—while small and inexpensive—had such value to my dogs because they were used regularly and were also a way to play and to be with me. Playing with the ball was something we did together, and it made them happy. Playing with the ball by themselves also provided stimulation so that they had an outlet to chew and to engage their interest and attention. Sammie especially loved using the tennis ball to give himself a back massage. He'd roll onto his back and sandwich the ball between his back and the ground. He'd then proceed to roll from side to side over the ball, all four legs in the air, white tummy exposed, and making satisfied grunts as the tennis ball massaged his back muscles.

Instead of accumulating items just to "have" them, my dogs had a few items that meant something to them, that they got a lot of use out of and that they cherished. Unfortunately for humans, we can feel pressure to work hard acquiring money so that we can have security and a nice life surrounded by beautiful things. Whilst that's not entirely bad, it can be if we become solely focused on that and motivated by it. As British philosopher, Bertrand Russell said, "It is the preoccupation with possessions, more than anything else that prevents us from living freely and nobly."

Life is not a competition, and it's not about material wealth. It's a spiritual journey to discover who we really are and to be the best versions of ourselves that we can be. That does not mean the richest, the thinnest, the most perfect. It's about being generous, grateful, contented, relaxed, self-aware, loving, and happy—happy in our own skin and in our choices. No one is perfect. We all have work to do to continue to improve our knowledge, our awareness, and our understanding; but work done to improve these aspects of ourselves is simply making the most of what we've been given—cultivating who we are not changing who we are.

Material things can weigh us down especially if we prioritise the gaining and retaining of material items over the development of our relationships with people, animals, and nature. When we concentrate on living a simpler version of our lives and avoiding material immoderation, we unburden our soul—we can be content with less and be richer because of it. The funny thing is that dogs seem to have this down already—they are happy, loving, and joyous. A dog doesn't care if its owner is rich or poor, what their owner looks like, or what social status they have. They don't care what car their owner drives or the square footage of their residence. A dog is only concerned with how it's treated and the relationships it has within its "pack."

My boxers are four-legged reminders that I need to lead a simpler life and concentrate on the important things. To concentrate on doing activities that really nurture my soul and bring happiness rather than damage the bank balance. Dogs are smarter than we give them credit for sometimes. They seem to have unlocked the secret that we spend so many years of our lives trying to—how to keep life simple and pleasurable, which leads me to my next life lesson . . .

LESSON 7

Do What Makes You Happy

WHAT MAKES A boxer dog happy? Anything and everything! For Max, being happy is bouncing around the backyard chasing his red cricket ball (very kindly donated by the neighbours), sitting with Andrej and me on the couch at night, waiting for a nibble of cheese after I make a sandwich, or walking with me or Andrej through the park. It's all the little things that he derives joy from.

One of my favourite dog quotes comes from Ambrose Bierce, "The most affectionate creature in the world is a wet dog," which is true for most. But when it comes to Max, I would have to argue that the most affectionate creature in the world is Max before his daily walk. He gets so happy before his walk and incredibly friendly, as if he's thanking me in advance for taking him out. I'm always amazed at how he seems to know that we're about to head out even though I don't say anything. I had made the previous mistake of teaching Sammie the word *walkies*, and it was always such a schemozzle trying to clip his lead to his collar while he was bouncing around after hearing the word. So with Max, I've never used the word, and yet he still accurately manages to figure out when I think it's time to go. Normally I will be sitting at the computer writing, and when I feel like I need a break, I'll get up and quietly go put my sneakers and some sunscreen on. Max could be sound asleep on the floor when I go to do those things, but when I return, he's sitting expectantly right next to his leash. When I grab it, he literally bounces a metre off the ground—his nimble and springy legs propelling him directly up into the air with all four legs bent up underneath him. His happiness erupts like a doggie jack-in-the-box.

Sammie and Towser derived joy from tearing around the yard at 5:00 pm every afternoon. They'd chase each other 'round and 'round in circles, sticking close to the fence line. They'd then turn about, and the other would chase for a while. Dirt and loose grass would be kicked up as they raced past. After five minutes of frantic activity, they'd both stop and lie down—completely satisfied with themselves. Why they did this every day at the same time, I have no idea. Probably just because it felt good, I suppose.

Sammie's other source of happiness was his daily ear rub. If I was sitting watching television or reading, Sammie would come and nudge his head into my hands. As I started to rub one of his ears, he'd lean in, close his eyes, and make low groans while intermittently wagging his tail. Apparently, there are so many nerves in a dog's ear that when triggered by touch, these nerves send pleasurable signals to the ear and to the internal organs as well. A wave of endorphins is released and fido (or in this case, Sammie) feels wonderfully happy, relaxed, and content. According to Dr. Allen Schoen, director of the Centre for the Advancement of Veterinary Alternative Therapies, Sammie was essentially "getting high on his own hormones" through his ear rubs.

When not making themselves happy, they make us happier. Dogs just know how to have fun—especially boxer dogs. Boxers are always on for a game, and they are generally just happy to either be with you or by themselves exploring the garden. If you're not around, they will always find ways to keep themselves entertained. Their sense of happiness can be contagious because you just can't stay cranky or upset when you see a boxer wagging its tail at you and bouncing around with ears propped up. When I see Max like this, it's almost as if he's saying, "Wanna play? Huh, do ya?" This is normally followed by him trotting off—lifting his front paws like a miniature prancing horse—to find his ball and bring it back to drop at my feet. Throwing the ball with him is fun because he enjoys it so much that I can't help but enjoy it too. His energy infects anyone in the vicinity.

ANGELA LEMANIS

Max's daily actions are a constant aide memoire that there is no better time to be happy than right now. Happiness comes from enjoying the moment and living it fully. But for some of us, happiness can be elusive—we have moments of happiness, bright sparks in time where we are completely cheerful, smiling, relaxed. Then we snap back (or get dragged back) into the real world and the daily grind.

I'm sure most of us are guilty or have been guilty of not appreciating the little things every now and then. I used to be so busy that I didn't even notice the little things—let alone appreciate them. I always seemed to be in a constant state of motion, the queen of lists, hastily moving from one task or appointment to the next. Once one was done, the next one was addressed, and when something was crossed off the list of things to do, another task was immediately added. Focus was shifted from one thing to the next thing with very little downtime to even recognise the achievement of completing the previous task. Being in this state of "what's next?" meant that I wasn't really aware of the things going on around me. I used to wear the term *time poor* like a badge of honour as if being that busy somehow meant that I was important and valued. Now I *know* how ridiculous that sounds.

It struck me one day, whatever happened to the kid who used to laugh and be silly? The kid who would sprint down the road just to feel out of breath? Who used to lie on the ground and stare at the clouds, trying to make animal pictures out of them, or who twirled round and round just to feel dizzy? I couldn't remember the last time I actually laughed until my stomach hurt. How had I managed to remove myself so far from the joy in life—the simple pleasures that put a goofy grin on your face or caused you to laugh so hard you'd snort? I remember once my brother making me laugh so much while I had a mouth full of chocolate milk that it ended up coming out my nose! My brother still has the ability to crack me up, but because we live in different countries, I don't get to see him as often as I'd like. When we were together growing up, we'd always play tricks on each other just for a laugh, but unfortunately life moves on, children become adults, and life has a way of becoming serious with responsibilities and demands. I guess I just stopped factoring fun into my schedule of things to do. I'm sure most people are so busy working, being parents, and building material lives that by the time they finish work, do the grocery shopping, wash the cars, mow the lawn, or whatever it is that is deemed important to get done every week, there doesn't seem like enough time left over to have fun.

What really has concerned me for some time is the number of unhappy and angry people there seem to be in the world these days. I read somewhere that anger is the result of not getting what you want. When someone does something that annoys us or upsets us, we get angry because it's not what we wanted to have happen. We wanted them to be more considerate or more aware of us and our feelings. But life isn't about getting what we want all of the time, and getting angry about things you can't control (like someone else's behaviour) just raises your blood pressure and induces a bad mood. Confucius says, "To be wronged is nothing unless you continue to remember it." And it's true. If you dwell on the thing that made you angry, you just feed it. The lesson is to move past it, control the things that you can and not sweat the stuff you can't.

Auckland traffic was one of the things I realised I couldn't control and therefore shouldn't internally rage about. It used to frustrate me to no end sitting stationary in the car, watching traffic lights change from green to red and green to red again without moving. After yet another change of the lights, I'd be lucky if the car inched forward half a metre. And it wasn't as if I could accurately predict when the busy times might occur. I would leave for work at the same time every day, and one day the traffic would flow quite well. The next day, it would be so congested it took forty-five minutes to travel three kilometres. The next day, it would be different again. There was no rhyme or reason to it at all. So there I would sit, anxiety levels creeping up, and I'd notice how frustrated other commuters looked as well.

One morning, I saw a driver looking like he was about to blow a gasket. His hands were thumping the steering wheel and he kept checking his wristwatch. Then I noticed his Golden Retriever dog in the back seat. His dog was having a great time—head out the window, looking at the people in the cars around him and the pedestrians on the street. He was sniffing the air and wagging his tail at the person sitting in the car nearby. I thought to myself that a situation that aggravated humans so much was a source of joy for him. He was in the car! He was with his owner instead of being left behind at home. What's not to like! When the car did start moving, he closed his eyes and raised his nose high into the air and let the wind wash over his ears and tongue.

It reminded me of Max during a recent car ride to the corner shop one sunny afternoon. He was in the back seat, and I had the window down just enough for him to stick his head out through. He spent the journey there with his head propped out and the fresh air filling his jowls so that

ANGELA LEMANIS

they billowed like the sails on a yacht. When we arrived at the store, he sat obediently in the seat awaiting my return so that he could feel the wind in his face again on the way home. Returning home the way we came, Max resumed his spot with his head out the window but every few minutes, he brought his head back inside and looked at me with such elation on his face it was as if he were saying, "You really should give this a try—it's *fabulous*."

Now when I am stuck in traffic, instead of worrying about the fact that I probably won't arrive at my destination on time, I breathe deeply in and out a few times and remind myself that the traffic situation is out of my control. I put my iPod on to a favourite playlist and make the most of my time in the car. I've learned that there's just no point in getting bothered about it anymore.

I don't know whether it is a result of our fast-paced lives or the Internet age we live in, but everything seems to need to be done yesterday and people are after immediate gratification. I was shopping the other day and the thought struck me, *I wonder how many people lay-by things these days?* I bet the number has dropped dramatically with the reliance on credit cards—so that we can put it on credit and have it now. When I was growing up, my parents said to me, "If you don't have the money for it, then you can't afford it." If it was something I really wanted, they would encourage me to lay-by the item and then use my allowance each week to pay it off. Obviously, we weren't talking about a lot of money, and I understand that now you need to build your credit rating in order to make large purchases like a house or a car, but I do believe the fundamental problem is that we have become so reliant on things happening immediately that we have created a messy problem for ourselves.

The more efficient we make work with new technologies, the more is expected of us. When email, Internet and mobile phones were introduced, the selling pitch was that these technologies would make our lives easier and more efficient, thereby freeing up time for work/life balance. The opposite has occurred. We are working longer hours and pumping out work to incredible deadlines. Now with mobiles being able to access us wherever we are, people can find us and make requests. Even if we are in our own personal time, the invasive nature of mobile phones means that you can be contacted anywhere, at any time—or at least people expect you to be contactable anywhere—and there are those who abuse this fact.

This need for immediacy is spilling over into our personal lives too. Weekends blur into months; months blur into seasons. We eat fast, talk fast, walk fast, drive fast—everything is disposable, and we often don't pay attention to our environment around us. How many car accidents have been caused by people talking on the phone or texting while driving, women putting makeup on in the car, and people eating or smoking while driving? Multitasking is not necessarily something to be proud of. To me, it just means that a situation that should have your complete attention—like driving—is now divided because you are adding other tasks to it.

And what is the result of all this immediacy and efficiency? A whole lot of unhappy, angry, and emotionally tapped-out people. Technology has made us move fast, and the downside is that we have lost ourselves in all of the so-called progress. Rates of depression and anxiety have soared, and the abuse of drugs and alcohol is reaching epic proportions. People are wanting to escape the warp speed of their lives and the added responsibilities and stress, by medicating themselves or drowning the pressure of their reality with drugs and alcohol.

Drugs and alcohol (like any addictive material) are instant gratification in themselves. I want to feel better, and I want it now! The trap for young players is that this kind of approach doesn't recognise consequences, and only covers up the real problem—the fact that you are desperately unhappy with some (or maybe most) areas of your life. Blurring the problem with drug abuse removes you even further from making the decisions that you need to make to improve your situation—that you need to slow down first and foremost so that you have time to assess your circumstances, change the things you don't like, deal with the perceived fear of making these changes, and become more authentic as a person.

Drug and alcohol addictions are glaring signs that someone is not happy and not coping. Addictions hide the real feelings behind momentary comforts. A fabulous quote from Mexican painter Frida Kahlo really sums it up nicely: "I tried to drown my sorrows, but the bastards learned how to swim." The only way out is through, and you need to work through these problems and come to terms with the root cause and then intentionally focus on making changes for the better.

Part of this is making the conscious decision to be happier. Happiness is a choice—a choice to think happy thoughts; a choice to be thankful for what we have; a choice to act from a place of happiness. We are responsible for our own lives so the focus should be on doing whatever it takes to make our life a good one. It takes time and a conscious effort, but small steps do make a difference. Celebrate yourself and your successes. Be grateful for the lessons garnered through mistakes. Be gentle with yourself and the thoughts you think about yourself. Don't judge or envy others for what they do or have. Identify potential sources that would otherwise have made you unhappy by identifying the root of the problem. Sometimes, we think we are unhappy about one thing, but the source of the problem is something entirely different.

My procrastinating behaviour used to make me unhappy with myself, but I discovered (when I sat down and thought about why I might be procrastinating) that it wasn't because I was lazy or slack (which is what I had originally thought about myself), it was that I didn't have a good grasp of what I was supposed to be doing and, therefore, was delaying the process because I didn't actually know where to begin. Once I had understood this, I could begin to address the problem and get moving. There was no reason for me to be unhappy with myself; I just had to identify the problem for what it actually was and either take action or let it go. Now if I am unhappy about a situation, I think carefully about what the problem is—what is causing me to feel this way and how can I address it? I'm also mindful of the fact that the problem isn't actually causing me to be unhappy. I can still choose to be happy in the face of this situation. After all, it's just a problem, and all problems can be fixed.

A sense of happiness does not come from external stimuli like success, wealth, power, or beauty. Happiness comes from within—not from something that can be taken away. As Deepak Chopra says, "When you depend on anything outside yourself to make you happy, your happiness is vulnerable." Ever wondered what it would actually take to be happy? Some would answer money because it would clear them of financial debt and the stress and pressure that brings. But money is not what would make you happy—getting rid of the stress and pressure would help, but those things will not make you happy either. All of us want our basic needs to be met, but once they are, excess doesn't make much difference—not where our sense of happiness and well-being is concerned. A great job and success might bring joy, but not true happiness. As Democritus the Laughing Philosopher said, "Happiness resides not in possessions, and not in gold; happiness dwells in the soul."

Another reason to be happier is that happy people are healthier people. According to a study published in the *Journal of Psychosomatic Medicine* by Carnegie Mellon University psychology professor Sheldon Cohen, "People who are happy, lively, calm, or exhibit other positive emotions are less likely to become ill when they are exposed to a cold virus than those who report few of these emotions." Similarly, in a published review from the Harvard School of Public Health, characteristics such as optimism and happiness were linked to a lower risk of heart and vascular disease and a quicker recovery from heart-related illness. Additional research also suggests that happier people live longer and are more productive. *Applied Psychology: Health and Well-Being* (2011) examined 160 studies, the results of which illustrated that happiness coupled with a positive outlook enhanced health. Pessimistic feelings, anger, and stress were linked to a higher risk of developing cardiovascular disease, inflammation, and a weaker immune system.

Happiness isn't just about wandering around all happy clappy for other people's benefit either. Studies have also shown that when it comes to happiness, we can't take a "fake it until you make it" approach. Slapping on a fake smile and pretending to be happy can actually lead to emotional exhaustion and leaves you feeling more miserable and upset than before you plastered on the phony grin.

There's no getting around the fact that we are only as happy as we believe ourselves to be. Being positive and content even if things aren't going our way is a choice. For me, I begin each day by thinking about all of the things I am grateful for—I call it my gratitude list. I'm grateful for my husband, my parents, my brother, my BFF Jenny, my wider family, my pets, my health, my sense of security, and all of the things that I cherish. This simple act has made an incredible difference to my attitude for the day. Instead of waking up and moaning about the day ahead, I begin in a positive frame of mind by appreciating and being thankful for everything that I do have now.

Even my quest for happiness makes me happier. The fact that I am consciously trying to lead a simpler, more valuable life brings a smile to my face. I'm certainly not without faults, and I can revert back to my old ways in moments of fragility, but I am on the right path for the most part. I've vowed to savour the small moments knowing that one day I might look back and realise the small moments were the most important and happiest ones of all.

ANGELA LEMANIS

LESSON 8

Be Who You Are

THERE IS NOTHING more bona fide, authentic or genuine, than a boxer dog. My boxers have never pretended to be anything they're not. They are who they are at all times—whether that be enthusiastic, obnoxious, crazy, naughty, sleepy, happy, or a combination of these. They don't cover their emotions, and when they feel their emotions, it's all in with 100 percent commitment. Their confidence is also endearing as they automatically back themselves in any situation, especially when meeting new people. They seem convinced that every person who meets them will immediately and absolutely fall in love with them.

Towser was always true to his nature no matter where he was or what he was doing. Being a pedigree purebred boxer and the son of an Australian champion show dog, Towser was blessed with beautiful colourings, markings, and proportions. When Towser was one year old, my father decided to enter him into a breed-specific conformation show. A conformation show is an interesting event that dog handlers and owners take very seriously. The American Kennel Club (AKC) describes the purpose of conformation shows as a means to determine which dogs meet the written requirements for the correct characteristics for that breed, including temperament, health, appearance, and physicality:

"For each breed the AKC registers, there is a breed standard which is a word description of the perfect dog of that breed. Standards describe the mental and physical characteristics that allow each breed to perform the function for which they were originated. The standard describes the dog's looks, movement and temperament. Breeders involved with each breed are attempting to produce a dog that most closely conforms to the breed standard," hence the name *conformation*.

In the show, boxer dogs of approximately the same age are paraded around a show ring and then stopped and "stacked" for judging. Stacking is the form a dog takes when in the show ring presenting to a judge—the head and tail are up, the front feet are square, the back feet extended behind, the chest is out, and the balance forward. The judge will run his or her hands over each dog checking the muzzle, the teeth, the bite and underbite, eye colour, the shoulder angles, depth of chest, and the slope of the dog's topline. Then the judge asks the handler to trot the dog "down and back," which involves the handler moving the dog in a straight line away from the judge to one corner of the ring, then returning in a straight line back to the judge.

Towser was in an age-group with fourteen other one-year-old puppies. He seemed to really enjoy the pampering that went into getting a dog ready to show and was especially intrigued with the talcum powder we placed on all of his white bits. He was in sensory overload as he watched Dad clean his paws, felt the smooth strokes of the brush on his back, sniffed the tissue that was cleaning the "goop" out of the corners of his eyes, and listened to the barks and whines of the other boxers at the show grounds. This was the first time Towser had seen so many other boxers in one place.

When showtime came, my father and Towser took their place second last in the line of dogs and handlers and followed as the line filed forward into the show ring. Dad was doing all of the right things in the initial run round the ring circle. Towser trotted obediently next to him, picking his paws up nicely and concentrating on what he was doing. Then it came time to "stack" and Dad bent down to arrange Towser's body into the correct pose, with his head high and his tail raised. While my father took the situation and his role as handler very seriously, Towser on the other hand had used what little stores of concentration he had in the initial run around the ring and was now over the whole thing. Instead of paying attention to Dad, he was happy to goof around trying to distract the other dogs and scheming to move away from the spot he was supposed to stand on.

Dad's head was still in the game, but he was well and truly on his own. When Dad raised Towser's head, Towser's tail went down. So Dad raised Towser's tail, and Towser's head went down. Dad placed Towser's back feet apart, and Towser's front feet moved out of place. The entire thing was comedy in motion, and Towser's body form remained completely fluid with no body part staying where it was supposed to be. It's not as if Dad hadn't practised this with Towser prior to the show. He had, but Towser's interest in anything and everything around him meant that all of the practice had gone out the window. While the other young dogs mostly managed to keep still as the judge examined them individually, Towser kept wanting to either sit, lie down, jump up on Dad, walk around in circles, or try to engage with the dogs in front of him and behind him.

Towser was just not the same as these young but somewhat trained show dogs—he was spontaneous, lively, and curious. The judge finally made it around to where Dad and Towser were. Towser was very excited to see this new person who was studiously intent on looking in his mouth, running his hands over his head and shoulders, and feeling his back legs.

Instead of standing still in the proper stacked pose, Towser was as fascinated at looking at all of the things the judge was. When the judge examined his mouth, Towser wouldn't stop licking the judge's hand. When running his hands over Towser's head and shoulders, Towser tried to sniff the judge's hands. When the judge moved to look at his back legs, so too Towser moved his head to peer around at what the judge was doing back there; and when the judge ran his hand up in between Towser's back legs to feel for two testicles, Towser's eyes bulged, his tail clamped down tightly, and his body jolted at the sudden intrusion. The look on his face suggested he was thinking, "Oy, what do you think you're doing back there?"

After the physical examination, the judge asked Dad to trot Towser down the ground and back again. When asked to perform this activity, the boxer's back should ideally be straight and the step should be strong and controlled, but there was nothing controlled about Towser's movement. By this stage, Towser had had enough of being kept in one spot, and when Dad tugged on his leash to move, Towser saw it as an opportunity to run like a wild thing. He took off with a surge, his body low to the ground and his muscular hind legs kicking out strongly, hauling Dad along behind him while Dad frantically tried to bring him back under control.

Poor Dad was struggling. Mum and I, on the other hand, were doubled-over in fits of laughter on the sidelines. Towser was all over the place—this way then that way, then intrigued by a piece of grass, then yawning, then excitedly barking at the other boxers. To say "scatterbrained" would be too light a term. The judge was very nice to him and obviously knew that Towser was young and it was his first show. He spoke to Towser in a soft tone, and Towser lapped it up—seemingly convinced that this judge thought he was absolutely beautiful. The judge must have seen something he liked because Towser received the encouragement award, but my family never entered him into another show.

Due to Towser's beautiful markings and proportions, as he grew up and matured, he had the ability to look regal and noble. Even when he was in his twilight years and his muzzle covered in grey fur and his back legs creaky, his disposition was majestic and refined and his eyes gallant, gracious, and kind. Towser was supremely beautiful, both inside and out.

He was also incredibly headstrong and didn't like being "called out" for doing something naughty. He knew when he'd done something wrong and would often approach apologetically before I'd even realised that he'd been up to something. When he behaved like that, he gave himself away, and either my parents or I would go looking for the result of his naughtiness. Upon finding it, we didn't have to do much more than say *no* because Towser already knew he'd been bad. He certainly was an individual, and my family and I loved all of his quirks because he wouldn't have been him without them.

Max is a completely different personality to Towser. Even though they share all of the common boxer traits, Max is a little more animated than Towser was. While Towser tended towards elegance as he matured, Max is rambunctious and madcap in his behaviour. He is of course, only three years old as I write this, so he might grow up a bit as he gets older, but I'm not expecting miracles. I think he will always verge on the threshold of nuttiness. But that's what I love about him and also what sets him apart from my previous boxers. His sheer enthusiasm spills over into all areas of his life. His enthusiasm isn't the only thing that spills over.

Max would have to be hands down the messiest eater I've ever seen. Food spills out of his jowls and all over my kitchen floor twice a day, seven days a week, three hundred and sixty-five days a year. Always being a finicky eater, Max will eat his mince straight away; but when it comes to the dry food, he'll pick it out of his bowl, lick it, and then spit some of it out. He also likes to go for a wander when he has a mouthful of dry food, so I'll have kibble bits trailing from one end of the kitchen to the other. Some of the dry food gets eaten, but the bits that fall on the floor are never picked up again—unless it's by me with a dustpan and brush. At first, it used to frustrate me exceedingly, but now I've accepted that it's just the way he does things, and I can actually laugh at the mess he makes now—especially when he's tried to eat brown rice. It will always be something that adds to his uniqueness and sets him apart from Towser and Sammie who both literally inhaled their food and licked their bowls to a spotless clean.

The thing I find most beautiful about dogs is that they are dogs. Yes, I'll admit to being a little shocked when I first witnessed Max secretly nibbling on cat poo (courtesy of the neighbour's cat who likes to poop in our garden bed) as if it were high-end caviar, and slightly horrified when Sammie re-ate the vomit he had just thrown up, or embarrassed when my dogs have unabashedly sniffed the crotches of strangers within mere seconds of meeting them, or perturbed when Max rolls around in dirt

ANGELA LEMANIS

minutes after having a bath, or nauseous when the very pleased Towser discovered a bone he had buried weeks ago and began to chomp on the green-tinged stinky thing again. While these behaviours don't fit with my idea of properness or good manners, my boxers are boldly and impenitently being who they are—they are acting like dogs. Dogs do that stuff, and no amount of reprimanding will change that. And nor should it. We don't get a dog as a pet so that we can "turn" it human. We get a dog because we want a dog, and all that comes along with that. Whilst dining out on cat poo, munching on a rotting bone, and rolling in dirt aren't my idea of a good time, dogs are going to do it whether we like it or not. They are simply, authentically, and confidently being true to their nature.

If only I could have been that confident when I was younger. The carefree and confident behaviour of my boxers made me think about the times I undermined my own sense of confidence and uniqueness with negative thinking.

I spent a large portion of my childhood trying to change myself in order to fit in; either trying to be what others wanted me to be or wishing I was someone else. From seven years of age, I remember wishing I was someone else. I wanted to be like my best friend at the time, Sarah. She was pretty and talented and everyone liked her. She was opposite to me in every way—she had tanned skin, blonde hair, and blue eyes. I had incredibly fair skin which was prone to freckle, dark brown hair, and green eyes. As a teenager, I remember buying women's magazines and seeing these gorgeous models staring back at me from the glossy pages. In the eighties (when I was a teenager), it was the era of the supermodels and the look of the day was tanned skin and blonde hair like Elle McPherson, Christie Brinkley, Kathy Ireland, Claudia Schiffer, and Linda Evangelista. I would look in the mirror, and I could almost see my self-esteem deflate before my eyes as I realised that I didn't (and wouldn't ever) look like these girls. What I didn't know at the time was that even these girls didn't look like that (thanks to the wonders of air-brushing and photo retouching). Not that it would have made a difference. All I knew was that I was different . . . and not in a good way.

I didn't have the skin that could handle being exposed to the sun at the beach, and fake tan wasn't invented yet so going to the beach was a cringe-worthy experience and one that I stopped doing once I turned fourteen, because I couldn't stand the taunts from friends about how I was so ghostly white that they would need to put their sunglasses on in order to look at me. Feeling that my appearance was somehow odd, I automatically wished I could look like the rest of my friends in order to fit in. Twenty-something years on, I am now grateful for my pale skin and the fact that I kept it out of the harsh Australian sun when I was younger.

In my twenties, I could list several things about myself that I would change, but this time it wasn't just about appearance. I wished I felt more confident in social settings like my friend Jenny who is adept at being able to talk to anyone about anything and never suffers from awkward pauses in conversation. I wished that I was funnier—quicker off the mark with a witty remark, perfectly timed repartee, or well-delivered joke—or that I always knew the right thing to say in any situation like my mum does. Instead of acknowledging what I did have and what I did do well, the little voice inside my head was always nit-picking on the negatives.

Hindsight is a wonderful thing. I can now see how pessimistically I thought and acted, but at the time, I was unaware of how much I beat myself up. I'd been guilty of making the age-old mistake of tying my self-esteem and self-worth to my appearance or to my personality—I was even guilty of tying my identity into my work and believing that a job defined me. I had an illuminating moment when I was walking Max one afternoon. Earlier that day, I had applied for a job and emailed my curriculum vitae (CV) to the owner of the company. I wrote a letter explaining why I wanted the job and finished it by saying that my CV was attached in the email so that they could get a better idea of who I was. I wrote it without thinking, but as I walked through the park with Max a few hours later I thought, *What a lie—that CV doesn't really tell the owner anything about who I am, but rather what I had done.* As I pondered this, I also had to think whether that was how I saw myself? Did I judge myself by what I'd done? Sadly, the answer was *yes*. That CV wasn't me. Especially seeing as everything I had worked for in recent years and included in that CV was everything I was trying to get away from. I didn't want the stress, the cramped little cubicle, the sickly fluorescent light, the air-conditioning that seemed only to spread the flu around to all floors of the building. I didn't want any of that, and I was applying for a job that didn't include any of that for that very reason. So why would I write that the CV would give any idea of who I was? It's a mistake I think so many of us make though. We spend so many hours, days, and years, working and climbing the ladder that we relate to that as who we are rather than what we do. Some of us literally become our work—we are defined by it, haunted by it, excited by it, a slave to it. It's no wonder then that when some people retire, they have such a void it's

ANGELA LEMANIS

almost impossible to fill with another activity because in a sense, part of their identity has gone.

To be who you are, you have to forgive yourself for the things you didn't do quite right. You need to really understand that life itself is a lesson and that we are constantly learning. Mistakes are part of learning. We are not always going to get everything right—no matter how hard we try to. We will make bad choices, do stupid things, act impulsively, and say hurtful things in a moment of anger or defensiveness. We have to forgive ourselves for that, learn from it, and then move on. My friend Jenny has always said, "I don't believe in regrets." And at first, I couldn't understand that. I had my regrets, and I was always amazed that she didn't. But now I get it. It's not that she hasn't acknowledged that she's deviated from her true path a few times; it's that she doesn't let these moments have a hold over her. She learnt from her mistakes and then moved on. She had the ability to see the mistakes for what they were—learning lessons. When you shift your mind-set to believing that mistakes are actually helpful (by making you more aware of yourself and your choices), then you can forgive yourself for them and then forget them. No guilt, no disappointment, no nagging voice telling you that you should have known or done better, no internal resentment—none of that. There's a freedom in that kind of thinking.

Being who you are also requires a certain amount of trust in yourself. If you don't trust yourself to be who you are and believe that you are uniquely magnificent and worthy, then you won't be able to fully connect with others. Being who you are means believing in yourself, believing in your actions and intentions—that all of it is coming from a place of truth.

I've learned to tell that little nagging voice in my head, that says I'm not good enough, to bugger off. If it can't say nice things about me, then it shouldn't be saying anything at all. It's never good to be judgemental—of yourself or others. Funnily enough, we often seem to be more accepting of others than we are of ourselves. Sometimes we have to get out of our own way and give ourselves a break. Concentrating only on the things you think you don't have prevents you from seeing and realising the things you do have.

Being comfortable with being me is one of the most important life lessons I've learned. Now I just try to be the best version of myself that I can be—kind, healthy, nurturing, forgiving, enthusiastic and hopeful, towards myself and others as well. These are the elements that make up the best me possible. I will let myself be me and will continue to enjoy my boxer dogs for being their wonderful doggie selves.

LESSON 9

Love Is All You Need

TOWSER, SAMMIE, AND Max really showed me the meaning of unconditional love—which is essentially what every dog does. Dogs have this beautiful ability to appreciate you just the way you are. I believe that dogs really "see" you—they sense your moods, they pay attention to your body language, and they listen to you (even though they have no idea what you're talking about). My three boxers would often sit there, heads cocked to the side, eyes focused on me with great intent as if they completely understood and wholeheartedly agreed with everything I was saying.

Because dogs can't talk, they show their love actively in the little things they do—the wonderful welcomes with enthusiastically waggy tails, the playful nudges, and the extent to which their eyes light up when you enter the room.

You really see how much your dog loves you when you come home after being away. Max never fails to greet me with buoyant exuberance every afternoon when I return home from work. So much so that on the car drive home, I find myself looking forward to the impending interaction. After watching me park the car in the driveway, Max makes a beeline for the back door and waits for me to let him in. Living in Auckland means that a lot of the time, it would have been raining while I'd been away, and I would invariably have to wipe his paws before letting him into the house. Even this ritual became an opportunity for Max to show his affection towards me. Before opening the door, I'd grab two towels: one for the floor and one to wipe Max's paws. When ready, I'd throw open the door and Max would spring in and immediately lift his front left leg and wait for me to wipe his paw gently with the towel before dropping his left paw and lifting his right one for a wipe. When they were done, he'd inch forward so that his back feet were on the towel and we'd repeat the process until all paws were clean and accounted for. While I concentrated on removing all remnants of dirt and damp, Max would wait for precisely the right moment when my face was closest to his to plant a big lick on my cheek as if to say, "Hi there." He never once missed an opportunity!

Due to Andrej's work schedule, he'd frequently arrive home after I did, and I could see Max getting restless and antsy at the time Andrej would normally turn up. Max would purposefully listen for the cars on the street, and he always seemed to hear our car well before Andrej pulled into the driveway. Knowing that Andrej was just outside, Max would sit patiently at the door with his chest puffed out as if holding his breath in anticipation of Andrej's entrance. As soon as the front door keys went into the lock and clicked open, Max would turn on the doggie charm—spinning 'round and 'round in circles, tail wagging, and head bobbing up and down. A furry brown welcome party of one.

While these daily greetings were well worth waiting for, the best reception we've ever received was after Andrej and I returned from a two-week holiday in the United States. Max was two years old at the time, and it was his first experience of a boarding kennel. I did my research to find one that came highly recommended, and three weeks before we were due to leave for our trip, I drove the forty-five minutes to the kennel with Max to see it firsthand and to meet the people who would be looking after him. The boarding kennel seemed very nice: it had clean, spacious kennels and offered great outdoor areas for play and exercise. The staff made a fuss of Max as he sniffed and thoroughly investigated the new surroundings.

When the day of our departure arrived, Andrej and I packed everything Max would need for his stay—his beanbag, food and water bowls, dog coat for keeping warm at night, and several dog toys. Max bounced into the car and settled into his spot on the back seat, ready for the journey.

Ten minutes into the ride, Max fell asleep. When we arrived at the boarding kennels, he leapt out of the car and stood next to me while Andrej went into the reception area to let the staff know we were there. A young lady came out with Andrej to take some of Max's belongings into the kennel and then came back to collect Max. Andrej and I gave Max a generous rub around his neck to say good-bye, but we didn't want to make too big a deal of the situation in case Max got anxious. As Andrej and I stood watching, Max happily wandered off with the staff member, and I watched his little butt sway side to side as he walked away. He didn't look back before he disappeared around the corner and was gone. On the drive to the airport, I wondered what he was doing and at what stage he would

ANGELA LEMANIS

look around for me and realise that I wasn't there. Would he worry that I wasn't immediately coming back to get him?

Meanwhile, Andrej and I were off on our much-needed overseas vacation. Our first destination was Boston where we did all of the "touristy" activities like visiting Fenway Park, roaming the Freedom Trail, picnicking in Boston Common, and shopping in Beacon Hill—all the while eating our fair share of clam chowder at the historic Boston Oyster House and drinking beer in the made-famous-on-TV Cheers Bar. From Boston, we tripped down to New York for a week before flying out to one of our favourite cities in the United States: San Francisco. Andrej had proposed to me in San Francisco several years earlier, and the city definitely held a magical place in both of our hearts. We rode the cable cars, walked the Golden Gate bridge, visited Fisherman's Wharf, ate breakfast at Mama's, and indulged in the heavenly crab cakes at the Buena Vista Cafe.

Even though we were having a fabulously relaxed time, my thoughts often turned to Max and how he was getting on.

The staff at the kennel sent regular emails to let me know that Max was doing just fine and settling in well, and as much as I wanted to believe them, a cynical voice in the back of my mind was saying, "Well, what else do you expect them to say? He's doing terribly and hating every second of it?" I knew they were probably telling me what I wanted to hear so that I could enjoy my holiday and not worry, but I hoped he was doing as well as they wrote. The only thing that did set my mind at ease was that the couple who owned the boarding kennel were a registered veterinary nurse and a veterinarian. If anything went wrong, they had my permission to do what was necessary to look after Max's welfare.

As our holiday drew to a close, instead of being sad the experience was over, I found myself sitting in Los Angeles airport waiting to board our Qantas flight silently energised by the thought of seeing Max again. The thirteen-hour flight from LA was long and tiring. I never could sleep well on planes, but after clearing customs in Auckland and heading to the car park, there was a renewed spring in my step in eagerness of the cheery reunion that awaited us.

Pulling into the car park at the boarding kennel, I shot out of the car before Andrej had time to turn it off. I jogged the short distance to the reception area and greeted the girl at the front desk. She sent another staff member to collect Max's beanbag and belongings while she gave me a quick summary of how Max had been while we were away. Apparently, he had played well with other dogs, ate all of his meals, slept well, and generally seemed to be in good spirits. Andrej collected Max's belongings from the staff member and went to put them in the car while I waited impatiently for Max to make an appearance.

I could hear the jangle of his collar and the *plop, plop, plop* sound of his footsteps on the polished linoleum floor before I saw his face. I held my breath as Max's reddish-brown figure rounded the corner with the staff member in tow. Max was looking down at the ground and didn't see me at first. I couldn't wait any longer, and I yelled excitedly, "Hi, Max." He looked up and saw me and immediately leapt forward in my direction—only constrained by the length of his leash. His mouth dropped open, his tongue hung out, and there was an animated glint in his eyes. As he got closer to me, his entire rear end bent forward so that he was walking sideways. Max's tail was vigorously wagging, and when he got to within one metre of me, he lurched out and jumped up, his front paws landing on my torso so that his face was just lower than mine.

"Hello, Max," I said again in a high-pitched tone, and he tried to lick my face. At that moment, Andrej returned from packing Max's things into the car and got a similar reception as Max immediately turned his attention to the alpha male of the house. Plenty of patting and neck rubbing later, Max settled in next to us as we paid the account, thanked the kennel staff for their great care, and wandered out towards the car. All my feelings of guilt at having left him were gone as he showed his happiness at our reappearance. Max didn't seem to care where we'd been, he was just ecstatic that we were back.

I once read a quote from American news commentator and writer Andy Rooney that stated, "The average dog is a nicer person than the average person." Writer Leslie Garrett concurs, saying that "it's a standard achieved without self-help books, life coaches, or religion. Turns out that what we love most about our dogs is their humanity. Something we find decidedly lacking in many humans." Thinking about the myriad of ways that dogs show their love and kindness to us, dogs do, through their actions, bring out the humanity in humans; and that's why people like having them around. We like who we are when they're around.

I remember having a small disagreement with my dad over lunch one day when I said that I thought dogs were actually more evolved than humans, to which my dad almost choked on his sandwich. "Oh yeah, how do you figure that?" he asked evenly, but the look on his face suggested he thought I was speaking absolute twaddle. I explained that dogs are more evolved because they don't hold grudges; they don't feel anxious about the future or guilty about the past; they live in the moment; they see most things through loving eyes; they don't get bogged down in regrets; they don't procrastinate, beat themselves up, pity themselves, or exhibit any of the other issues or hang-ups that the majority of us humans are plagued by every now and then. *Compelling argument*, I thought. Apparently not, as Dad countered, "That's because they're not as intelligent as we are and, therefore, don't have the capacity to understand those things." Well, hey, if that's the case, then ignorance is bliss. I think the dogs have got it right!

A beautiful demonstration of how accepting dogs are happened when I was six years old. The next door neighbour had a three-legged Irish Red Setter dog named Prince. I would sit in the backyard and watch Prince as he played on our quiet suburban street with the other neighbourhood dogs. He'd sprint as hard as he could, chasing a couple of the dogs before turning and being chased. They'd all wrestle on the ground and play fight noisily. Prince played as hard and fast, and with as much gusto, as the dogs with four good limbs. He didn't waste time looking enviously at them wishing he had four, he was simply happy to be part of it. Similarly, the dogs that had four good legs didn't look on in pity or judgement of him for only having three legs. They accepted his difference and included him in the game without delay. Unfortunately, we humans are one of a few species that has been known to bully or pity others based on appearance, age, disability, or any slight difference. We can certainly learn from dogs how to be more accepting of and loving towards others.

Dogs are compassionate creatures that seem to return love and affection easily. In fact, dogs will love humans even if they are cruel to them.

After Sammie had passed away, I made the decision to volunteer at the Auckland Society for the Prevention of Cruelty to Animals (SPCA). After taking the Animal Village Volunteer course, I became a canine volunteer in the "doggery"—the place where all of the rescued newcomers go until they have passed their temperament and health assessments—and was tasked with cleaning pens, feeding the dogs, bathing and walking the dogs, and looking after the quarantined puppies.

The doggery had lots of different characters—some were dogs that had been removed from dog fighting rings and others were being kept there because their temperament meant that they couldn't be adopted out. Some dogs were placed there to continue their recovery after they had been discharged from the animal hospital. I saw plenty of dogs that had been horrendously treated—abused, starved, tied up and left for dead, or subjected to fighting in dog fights. I found it astounding that even though some of these dogs had suffered at the hands of humans, they still trusted us. I was a complete stranger to these dogs, and yet they welcomed me with an enthusiastic tail wag. It didn't hurt that I brought them food too.

It almost broke my heart one day when I went to volunteer and was assigned to look after a young dog that had been mistreated. His little battered body was skin and bone (and he had to wear a coat because it was the middle of winter, and he literally had no body fat to keep him warm). His fur was missing in places, and his shoulder blades and hip bones jutted out glaringly. It was as if the skin had been draped straight over bone with no fat or muscle to provide cushioning. My first job was to take him out of his pen for a very short walk in the yard (just so that he could be outside in the sunshine for a while as opposed to exercise). When I entered his pen, despite not knowing me, he gave a wag of his tail as he gingerly wandered over to where I was. I thought to myself, *Here is a beautiful but damaged dog—damaged by a human whom he thought he could trust and who had let him down and hurt him—and yet he still has faith in me that I won't do the same.* That sense of trust and faith was admirable. This dog would have had every right to growl at me or cower in the corner away from me, but he didn't. Instead, he let me attach a leash to his collar and walked with me outside his pen and into the yard.

On the way out to the gardens, he had to stop for a piddle but was so weak he couldn't maintain his balance while lifting his rear leg. So he gently changed position to be closer to me, and when he lifted his left rear leg to piddle, he leaned over to the right so that his body was touching my legs. He leaned against me for support and balance while he finished piddling, and when he was done, he looked up at me with his dark brown, somewhat weary eyes, as if to say "thanks." I gave him a reassuring pat, and we continued to walk the short distance to the yard and spent the next half hour sitting on the lush green lawn, the sun beating down on us, his head resting in my lap, and me patting him and whispering encouraging words like, "You're a good dog." We stayed a bit longer than normal because I just felt he needed the extra love, attention, and kindness.

The SPCA is so vital to dogs like this, and the staff and volunteers truly love, care for, and respect the animals. The first time I saw this little dog, I was struck by how skinny he was, but I was even more surprised to hear from a member of the canine team that he had come in much skinnier, and it was only because he had been hospitalised and cared for by the SPCA that he'd put on enough weight to be able to leave the hospital and board in the doggery. I hate to think how he looked on the first day he was rescued, but the great thing was that once given the chance, he didn't take long to recuperate and begin his recovery. Every fortnight, I looked forward to seeing him and the steady progress he made. Each time I saw him, he'd put on a little more weight and his fur looked glossier. The fortnight after that, his weight continued to increase, and there was a new energy in his step and a glint in his eyes. Witnessing his recovery advance from fortnight to fortnight was wonderful, and after about two months of care and attention, he was a healthy and happy young dog about to be adopted by a lovely family who couldn't wait to take him home, show him his plush new dog bed and toys, and take him for walks to their local beach. This dog had moved from a state of utter despair to complete happiness because he kept the faith in humans that we weren't all bad. He was prepared to give our species a second chance. What a brave little dog indeed!

The trust that dogs place in humans can also be transformational as evidenced in the American Puppies Behind Bars programme, where the love from eight-week-old puppies has helped to soften the hearts of many a hardened criminal. The puppies are placed with inmates to be trained as service dogs for the disabled, including wounded soldiers. The puppies and prisoners spend all day every day together—with the puppies sleeping in crates in the inmates' cells—and close bonds are formed. Prisoners who've participated in this programme say that these tiny puppies give them something that many of them have never experienced before: real responsibility, trust, loyalty, and love. Some of these prisoners, who previously thought of themselves as "worthless", have been given a new outlook on life, thanks to their gentle and unassuming furry companions.

As a dog owner, I've spent many, many hours teaching my dogs obedience, skills, and tricks; but it took me a while to understand that the whole time I was with them, they were teaching me things too.

By following the simple lessons my dogs have taught me, I now actively demonstrate and give voice to how much I care for those I love. The smallest actions like greeting your loved ones with a smile and a welcoming display (a hug, a kiss), forgiving others their flaws when they make a mistake, accepting each other and our differences, being there to spend quality time with those you love, and being encouraging of their ideas and goals can mean so much to someone else and should never be underestimated.

The good thing about love is that it is specific. Your spouse loves you because of who you are. Your pets love you because they see you for who you are too. Your friends and family love you—not because they are supposed to, but because they want to. They love you for the good and the bad because they know that the good outweighs the bad nine times out of ten. That's such an incredible thing. Having someone you love tell you that you've done a good job, that they're proud of you or that they love you can make you feel invincible.

It is a sad fact that animal lives are much shorter than human lives, but I believe they make the most of their time with us by living each moment, loving unconditionally, trusting us, showing compassion, and being the best friends some of us will ever know. They pack their lives full of real emotions and, therefore, don't need to hang around this world as long as humans do. They know what it means to live in the limited time they have. They know that love is really all you need.

Be Present, It's a Gift

ALBERT EINSTEIN once said, "I never think of the future—it comes soon enough," and that it does. My problem was that I used to spend a lot of time and energy worrying about the future. I didn't even know I was doing it until I'd catch myself mid-thought worrying about a meeting that was three days away or worrying about how I was going to get out of a dreaded social event on the weekend. Sometimes I'd even be sitting watching TV, and I'd stop and think, *What was I just worrying about?* Then I'd remember, and I'd start worrying about it again.

My boxers have taught me not to be concerned with the future and to dedicate more time to living in the moment. Watching the behaviour of dogs, you realise that they are really "present" wherever they are, and they give their full attention to what they're currently doing. While I have often been intrigued about what Max thinks about when he sits on the back deck, looking out into the sky and sniffing the air, I'm sure he's not fretting about global warming, agonising over the current state of the health-care system, or speculating about whether the world economy will rebound anytime soon. When Max is out on the step, he's totally present, observing the environment around him, noticing the subtle change in light as the sun sets, listening to the neighbourhood sounds, and detecting the different scents on the air. Being present is a bit harder for us human-folk though because we tend to worry about what lies ahead and sometimes brood about what has been before. Sometimes it's the very existence of what has been before that scares us into making sure it doesn't happen again in the future.

Dogs aren't tied down by this stuff. They have a lighter heart because they don't worry that they might not be able to find the burial place of their favourite bone or that it might be rainy tomorrow. They don't sweat the things that happened last week. Sounds liberating, doesn't it? Well, it is. It takes a conscious effort to stop myself from worrying, but it can be done and is very enjoyable when I do achieve a state of presence.

I read once that to worry is to give all of your power to something you don't want to occur—the "what we fear, we create" concept. Why would we want to give power (or time) to something that we don't want to happen? And yet, we still do it. I was such a worrier that I used to think that if I didn't worry enough about a potential situation or worse-case scenario, I wouldn't be adequately prepared for that situation should it occur. But the ridiculous part is that I was making a plan to deal with something that probably wouldn't happen. By watching all of my boxer dogs over the years and seeing how they exist with a sense of freeness, I've tried to adopt the practice of being more present and letting go of the unnecessary worry and stress. Notice I wrote *tried* because I have yet to master it, but I have come a long way from my nail-biting anxiety about what "is to come." It's not easy, but it's definitely worth the effort.

I hear you protesting as I write this that it's easy for dogs to be present when their lives are so simplistic. Granted, the daily agenda for Max comprises of waking up, eating, playing, sleeping, walking, eating, contemplating life on the back step and sleeping. Not especially taxing or significant enough to incite wrinkle-causing, blood-pressure-elevating worry but then neither should our lives be. If we are that concerned about something in our lives, then maybe we shouldn't be involved in it. The concept is incredibly basic, and some may say *naive*—I can hear protests of "if only it was that easy"—but I do wholeheartedly believe that we make life much more complicated than it actually needs to be. And remember, sometimes the simplest notions are the hardest to achieve.

Being present also means slowing down for many of us. I think that in my case, the lack of presence was coupled with me trying to do too much in too little time.

When I was attending university in Townsville, I used to race home during the breaks in my lecture schedule and take Sammie for his daily walk. Sammie would be waiting to greet me when I came home because he knew it meant "walkies." I'd throw my bag on the kitchen counter, grab the leash, and head out to the backyard to get him ready to go. Trying to put the leash on him was a feat in itself as he would bounce around with unbridled excitement just out of reach for a good few minutes before he'd calm down enough for me to attach the leash to his collar.

Heading out through the gate, he'd be a good metre in front of me, straining at the end of the leash while I ineffectively cried "heel" to the back of his head. The beginning of the walk started with such gusto, but as soon as we drew near the first tree (which happened to be on the neighbour's

ANGELA LEMANIS

property), he'd stop, sniff, walk around, sniff the other side, and then lift his leg to piddle. The tinkle of piddle was followed by one further inspection to make sure his calling card had sufficiently covered the scents of the other neighbourhood dogs that had been there before him. The skill, concentration, and methodical approach that went into inspecting the tree and its smells would, I'm sure, have received approval from many a crime scene investigator. After a few minutes, Sammie would be back at the end of the leash, straining to get to the next tree so that he could repeat the process.

Needless to say, this detailed approach to his daily walk used to aggravate me to no end. It was as if he'd stockpiled his piddle just so that he could ration it out on every tree along his walking track. It was more of a piddle-fest and sniff-test than a walk! There were so many trees in our neighbourhood that it didn't matter which route we took, the stopping, sniffing, and piddling would have a walk that should have taken forty-five minutes last for well over an hour.

I remembered Mum telling me that when she used to walk Ben that he had all sorts of trouble peeing on trees. He was still quite young and squatted when he piddled, but one day, he sidled up to a tree so that his left side was closest to the tree's trunk. Mum was so surprised that he was going to try peeing like the big dogs, but her surprise soon turned to laughter when, after preparing himself and getting his balance sorted, he lifted the wrong leg, his right leg, and piddled towards where she was standing instead of on the tree. Unfortunately, he had not grasped the concept just yet. Sammie, however, had no problem in that department, and while I anxiously watched the clock and wondered whether we'd ever be finished in time for me to get back to university, he was relishing every minute of it. He was out of the fenced yard, he was with me, and he was in the big wide world where other doggies were. He thoroughly enjoyed this time, and yet because my mind was otherwise concerned with my afternoon schedule, I was frustrated.

I soon realised that he had the right approach to it though—living in the moment and making yourself be exactly where you are. I made the decision that I wasn't going to win this battle only to lose the war. If I'd made Sammie rush through his walk, it would only make him unhappy and then I'd feel guilty knowing that I hadn't provided him enough time to enjoy his one trip out of the yard each day. I resolved that when I was walking with Sammie, I was only walking with Sammie. I wouldn't check my watch. I wouldn't let my mind stray to my list of tasks or my schedule.

I would enjoy being with him and watching his wonder at the world. This meant a change in his walking times. Instead of during my breaks from study, we went out in the early morning which ensured enough time to leisurely wander the streets with him. Once I had slowed myself down and switched focus to being more present, I loved those walks just as much as he did. I was with my dog, we were in nature, and we were by ourselves—just my dog and me. Bliss!

LESSON 11

Give Others the Chance
to Surprise You

M Y BOXERS HAVE always been able to surprise me, which is nice because after all, surprise is the spice of life. Just when I think I know what to expect from the breed, and when I think I know my pet's personality enough to predict how he will react to something, he does something completely new and out of the blue.

One of these occasions occurred when Sammie was just over two years old. We lived next to a lovely lady and her husband and their elderly cat. Sammie and the aging (and somewhat grumpy) cat had a tense relationship. The cat had no patience with Sammie's overly enthusiastic energy and tendency to crash around—all legs and paws—and encounters with the cat would often end in Sammie receiving a swift swipe across the nose. The cat's grumpiness was more than likely the result of living with daily aches and pains. The cat suffered from an advanced case of arthritis and had difficulty walking, jumping, and finding a comfortable position to sleep in. One day though, the cat was noticeably lethargic and was having difficulty jumping up onto the couch that sat on the front porch of the neighbour's house, where he would usually sleep in the afternoon sun. Sammie was paying close attention, and after watching the cat's efforts from a distance and sensing that the poor old thing was having a particularly bad day, Sammie wandered over to where the cat was.

For the first time, Sammie approached the cat quietly and calmly, and for a few seconds, they eyed each other up—the cat trying to determine Sammie's motives, and Sammie judging whether the cat was going to object to his close proximity. Instead of the usual heated exchange, the cat turned to face the couch and tried to jump up onto it but didn't have the strength and collapsed back onto the ground. When the cat tried again, he managed to place his front paws on the seat cushion and to my absolute surprise, Sammie stuck his nose under the cat's bottom and gave him enough of a lift for the cat to be able to scramble his way onto the couch. These two enemies who enjoyed tormenting each other on a regular basis had called a truce. I watched in utter disbelief as the cat finally settled down to nap while Sammie lay down on the porch in front of the couch and rested too. He didn't go to sleep; he just lay there on the ground with his eyes open for almost half an hour before deciding that the cat was fine on his own. He then gave the cat a cursory sniff and wandered back to our place. If I hadn't seen Sammie do that with my own eyes I would never have believed it was possible. He only ever performed this act of service one time, but it was one of the cutest things I've ever witnessed.

As for the cat, after a course of treatment, the cat's mobility improved. The tense relationship the pair enjoyed before the temporary cease-fire was called was well and truly restored. Sammie went back to receiving a few more unwelcome hisses and narrow misses as the old cat chastised him for his jaunty presence. But for me, the surprise was in seeing how Sammie helped the cat during its time of need and how the cat had allowed him to help too.

It always amazes me to hear stories of dogs going above and beyond to help their friends and companions. Dogs are so generous with their care and devotion that they are as loyal to other animals as they are to humans. At the time of writing this book, there was a touching story about a black Labrador dog that stayed by its companion—a yellow Labrador—after it had been struck and killed by a car on a busy Los Angeles County freeway. The black Labrador stood guard over the yellow Labrador's body, making sure no other cars hit it until someone was able to remove it safely from the road. Meanwhile, another Labrador named Hawkeye demonstrated his unyielding devotion by lying down on the floor beside his deceased owner's coffin at the funeral service. His owner, Navy SEAL Jon Tumilson—who was posthumously awarded the Purple Heart and Defence Meritorious Service Medal—died in a helicopter crash while serving in Afghanistan. Images taken at Mr. Tumilson's funeral show the faithful Labrador retriever lying within a few feet of his owner's flag-draped coffin.

Another heartwarming story of loyalty hailed from Massachusetts, USA where a female eight-year-old pit bull named Lilly pulled her owner out of the way of an approaching freight train. Lilly's owner had fallen unconscious onto the train tracks, and Lilly leapt into action, dragging her owner off the tracks to safety, just before the train thundered past. Lilly's owner was unharmed, but Lilly wasn't as lucky. She was struck by the train and sustained a fractured pelvis, internal injuries, and severe trauma to her right front leg, which needed to be amputated at the veterinary hospital. After several operations, Lilly's future looks good, and she is back at home with her family. Lilly put her own life at risk in order to save her owner, which is the ultimate display of love, loyalty, and devotion.

It's often said that a dog is man's best friend, and if these stories aren't proof enough, the surprising new things we are now discovering about how our fur buddies can help us will further substantiate the point. Dogs have always been beneficial to our health by helping to lower blood pressure and stress levels, improving depression, and reducing anxiety; but recent studies now reveal that dogs can also detect cancers and other serious diseases in humans.

The canine sense of smell is incredibly sensitive (up to 100,000 times more so than ours) and can be very accurately used to detect illness in humans. There are actually bio-detection dogs that are being trained to sniff out cancer from smelling the breath or urine samples of humans. In studies conducted by researchers in Germany (using a programme developed by the Cleveland Clinic), dogs were trained to smell a patient's breath, searching for the odour that is associated with lung cancer. These dogs accurately identified cancer 93 percent of the time. Dogs have also been trained to recognise bowel cancer, breast cancer, and bladder cancer with stunning accuracy. They are able to do this by recognising the small changes in smell that comes from unhealthy tissue. Dogs have also been trained to sense changes in behaviour, like epilepsy dogs or seizure-alert dogs, that can sense an oncoming seizure in their owner anywhere from a few seconds before the seizure occurs to forty-five minutes before the onset of the attack. Other smart dogs can discern when a diabetic's blood sugar level peaks or drops, can help sufferers of narcolepsy by barking or pawing at them before the onset of sleep paralysis, and can pick up the early stages of a migraine.

Max is by no means trained for anything other than to sit, stay, come, and down; but one night, he understood that I was in pain. A migraine had managed to creep up silently on me like a cranial ninja, and by the time I realised it was a migraine and not a standard headache, it was too late. The throbbing pain—which was moving from awful to intense—had taken the whole left side of my head captive and was especially concentrated around the back of my left eye. I took some pain relief, but the migraine had well and truly settled in, and I was feeling nauseous and incredibly sensitive to any form of light. I took myself off to the darkness of the bedroom, seeking the comfort of a soft place to lie down. Max came with me as he usually does at bedtime, but instead of sleeping at the foot of the bed, he lay horizontally across the bed and gently put his head on my chest and looked up at me. It was as if he was trying to comfort me by letting me know he was there if I needed him. He stayed that way until I finally managed to drift off to sleep and was still in the same position the next morning when I woke up.

He acted in a similar way when I had all of my wisdom teeth removed. Because the lower molars were more problematic to remove than the upper ones, I had to undergo a general anaesthesia in hospital and have all of them removed at once with the help of my very skilled oral surgeon. When I came home, my head was wrapped in an ice pack bandage, my face was swollen, I couldn't talk (because I had also received a local anaesthesia into my bottom lip area), and I was still a bit groggy. My husband got me comfortable on the couch and gave me the remote control. As soon as I was settled, Max came and lay down next to me very gently and stayed there until I fell asleep. Dogs care about us, and they show this when they sense we are in pain. It just goes to show how in tune our dogs are with us and how much they pay attention to any changes in our body language or behaviour.

There are so many stories out there that tell of the loyal and nurturing nature of dogs—from dogs that have either stayed by their injured owner's side until help arrived or notified others that their owner needed rescuing. The stories are many and varied, but all serve to show us that a dog's love, dependability, and allegiance shouldn't be underestimated.

Max is exceptionally loyal. He often keeps tabs on me and where I am in the house and will, most times, be right beside me as I move around the place. It was on one such occasion that I tested him to see if he was as quick at keeping tabs on me as Towser and Sammie used to be.

Max was walking beside me as I wandered from room to room with the clean laundry I had just folded and was in the process of putting away. When Max left my side to walk down towards the front door, I hid behind the bedroom door and waited for him to come back down the hallway. He loped down the hallway and walked into the bedroom looking for me. When he didn't find me, he left the room and headed towards the second bedroom. I heard his footsteps on the polished wooden floor of the second bedroom and listened quietly as he walked from the second bedroom to the third bedroom. When he didn't find me there, I noticed a change in his footsteps. Instead of walking, he was now trotting from room to room—double-checking to see if he had missed me there. He came back into the main bedroom and ran straight past my hiding spot into the ensuite bathroom. There was a sense of desperation in his search, and he came back out from the ensuite and stood in the bedroom listening. It was at that moment that I jumped out from behind the door and surprised the bejesus out of him. His surprise quickly turned to relief as he bounded over to where I was—happy to have located me. Unbeknownst to him, he had just had his first lesson in the game of hide-and-seek.

I had played this game with Towser and Sammie, and both of them loved the adventure of the search and the thrill of finding me crouched behind something. I would make such a fuss of them, and they'd seem very pleased with themselves for their tracking and finding skills and knowing that they had done exactly what I wanted them to. Towser, Sammie, and Max all demonstrated patience by sitting in the kitchen obediently, while I went off to hide somewhere. Even though they would tremble with anticipation, they'd wait for the signal—a whistle—which meant they could come and find me. Normally, they found me fairly quickly because I always made the first hiding place quite easy, like behind a door or something. As the game went on, I would hide in more secretive spots and see how long it took them to find me. I had to keep changing it up and finding new places to hide because they would always remember where I had hidden before and would go back and check each place to see if I was there again. One of the best hiding places I found was in the pantry behind a closed door because it meant that they would have to use their sense of smell as well. When they located me, they'd often snort noisily at the gap underneath the pantry door, and that was my cue to fling open the door and yell, "Good boy!"

Andrej and I would also play outdoor hide-and-seek with Max at the park. Andrej would capture Max's attention while I sneaked off and hid behind a tree or a shrub. When I was settled in my hiding spot Andrej would say to Max in a high-pitched tone, "Where is she?" "Where did she go?" Max would immediately begin looking for me around the park. If he got too far off the scent, I'd either whistle or call his name so that he had a hint, and in no time he'd find me. The celebrations that ensued were the epitome of happiness—Max would twirl round in circles, tail wagging, tongue hanging out, and a few *ruff, ruff* barks were thrown in for good measure—all demonstrations of his joy at knowing he'd done a good job.

To all the dog owners out there, I highly recommend teaching your dog how to play hide-and-seek. Once they understand the rules of the game, they absolutely love it. It gives your dog physical and mental exercise; engages their senses of sight, smell, and hearing; and provides them with a game that rewards them at the end when they find you. It's a game that you can play over and over again—either indoors or out—and as long as you find new places to hide, your dog will never grow tired of playing it with you.

Max is so used to playing hide-and-seek with me now that if I disappear when he's not looking and give a quick whistle, he automatically changes into seeking mode and comes looking for me. I'm always surprised at how he is always on for a game and how happy he is when he finds me. To see him that thrilled, always puts a smile on my face, and I know we will still be playing the game as enthusiastically when he's ten years old. I might have to move into a new place by then though as I am quickly running out of hiding places in our current house!

The element of surprise is elementary (my dear Watson). As with my notions of believing I know my dogs inside out, I often think I have people all sorted out too. I've made the mistake of thinking that I'm a good judge of character, and in most cases I am; but what I've learnt is that people have many layers and even though we might get to see most of those layers, we don't always get to see them all. Just when you think you know someone, they can surprise you.

A wonderful quote about surprise came from Francois de La Rochefoucauld and states that "the only thing that should surprise us is that there are still some things that can surprise us." It's no secret that appearances can be deceiving. I realised one day that people aren't as bad as I thought they were. I used to say to myself, "I hate people," when someone did something unnecessary, something cruel, or something hurtful. It's all about context. What I now realise is that people are just trying to get through the day. We often don't really see people for who they are. We make snap judgements about what they've said or done, but do we actually think about the individual really? Are they scared, feeling uncomfortable in this situation, feeling out of their depth? Do we stop and think about what actually lies behind someone's behaviour? Do we bother to separate the behaviour from the person? Everyone is capable of behaving badly every now and then. But do we stop to put any of it in context? What are they holding under the surface that we don't know about because they choose not to reveal that to us?

All of us have something that we keep private for ourselves to deal with, figure out, mull over, or hide. Humans are social creatures, but we don't share everything. And it's in the midst of choosing what we do put on

ANGELA LEMANIS

display and share with others and what we keep for ourselves that forms the public persona of who we are—the face we put on for others to see. And it's that persona that we are often judged by and that we make judgements of others by as well. We take a snapshot of someone at a point in time, and then define them by it.

There's a school of thought regarding the way we negatively judge others that suggests that, more often than not, the negative qualities we recognise in others are the qualities we don't like about ourselves. Carl Gustav Jung, a Swiss psychologist and psychiatrist who founded analytical psychology, believed that if there was anything we wished we could change in others, we should first examine whether it is not something that could better be changed in ourselves. He also said that "everything that irritates us about others can lead us to an understanding of ourselves." His theory that people with similar character traits can recognise those same traits in others strongly aligns with the old proverb "It takes one to know one."

If you give people the chance, they will often surprise you, and mostly in a good way. Have you ever had a situation that seemed overwhelming, and the person that came to your aid was the person you least expected? This surprised you because you had pigeonholed that person into a certain box with a neat little label on it because you believed that, based on past experiences, he or she wouldn't be the one that you would consider helping you out in this situation. Surprise! They did.

The problem with judgements, boxes, and labels is that unless we reassess these frequently, we continue to believe that the person (we have previously labelled) is only capable of acting and behaving inside the boundaries of that label. By putting people in boxes, we are saying that we don't think they can be anything else. People are complex and complicated and deep and wonderful and kind and difficult and generous and perplexing and, and, and . . . .

We can be all of those things at any time, but we are not limited to those alone and therefore shouldn't be defined by those alone. I know that I'm still discovering things about myself all the time, but I know that there are people out there who still have a label for me that is "so five years ago!" Not that I mind, but it does make me think about how I might have labelled others in the past.

Some say that when something terrible happens, you soon find out who your friends are. That's because the ones that step forward in a given situation may not be the ones you expected, and the ones that desert you are the ones you thought would stick by you through anything. It is hard not to make initial judgements about people based on their behaviour, but the good thing about snap judgements and even more firmly entrenched pigeonhole beliefs is that they can be changed. All I can say is give people the chance to surprise you—you will be amazed at what you might discover.

ANGELA LEMANIS

LESSON 12

Through the Looking Glass: the Importance of Following Your Curiosity

CURIOSITY MAY HAVE killed the cat, and it's nearly claimed a couple of boxer dogs over the years, but that's never stopped my dogs from following it. Just as Alice went through the looking glass into another world, my boxers' healthy sense of curiosity led them to new experiences and a new sense of wonderment. Curiouser and curiouser indeed!

Boxer dogs are perpetual puppies. Even when they grow old, they still have that puppy playfulness. This can, of course, get them into trouble every now and then. Max has always had a knack of getting into every nook and cranny in the backyard—investigating every fence post, every plant and shrub, every pebble. One day, about a year after I got Max, I arrived home from work to find him sitting in his usual spot at the back door, waiting for me to let him in. But this day, there was something drastically different about the sight that greeted me. Max was covered in golf-ball-sized bumps, from the top of his head to the tip of his tail. There wasn't an inch of fur untouched by a lump. I was shocked—my one-year-old puppy resembled a monster from a scary movie. In an immediate panic, I grabbed the phone from the kitchen counter, snatched the vet's business card from underneath the magnet on the fridge, and dialled while I rushed to open the back door. It was late, and I didn't know if the vet was still there or whether I'd have to dash off to the after-hours clinic instead.

"Please, vet," I pleaded under my breath, "please, please, please be there."

"Hello, Shore Vets," a pleasant voice said down the phone line.

"I've just come home to find my dog covered in large bumps," I blurted back, "Can I bring him in to see the vet now?"

Yes, I could and should bring him in immediately—the vet would wait until I got there. As I opened the back door and bent down to look at my lumpy bumpy puppy, Max came whirling in, tail vigorously wagging back and forth. He licked my face and bounced around the kitchen. He certainly seemed normal enough "personality-wise," but his fur was horrendous. I touched one of the bumps, and it was hard underneath his skin. I picked him up, grabbed his leash and my bag, and headed for the car. Thank goodness the vet's office was only a five-minute drive from home and the peak-hour traffic had died down for the night. In the front seat, an unfazed Max had his head stuck out the window, licking at the evening air as it rushed by.

The local veterinary practice is operated by two vets who share the workload. One is a calm and gentle lady whose love of dogs oozes through her pores. As well as being one of the vets, she also runs regular puppy socialisation courses and provides answers to all sorts of erratic dog behaviours and their causes—a female Cesar Millan, if you will. The other vet is a quietly spoken man who is very thorough in his methods and is always helpful in answering the many questions I had concerning Max's well-being. Tonight, it was our lady vet who was in residence. As Max and I walked in through the front door, she took one look at him and said, "Oh dear, that doesn't look good. You'd better come right in."

After running a litany of checks, including Max's first experience with a rectal thermometer which saw his eyes expand to the size of saucers and his ears prop up when inserted, the vet deduced that he'd had a severe allergic reaction to "something."

Hmm, a bit vague, but I'll go with it, I thought. She was one step ahead of me. As she plunged a particularly large needle into a glass vial of medicine, she ran through a list of plants that could potentially cause this type of reaction, but I didn't have any of those in my backyard. With that crossed off, she quizzed me on any potential poisons that he could have stumbled upon and ingested, but all of our chemicals were kept safely out of reach in our garden shed. Next, we discussed whether we'd sprayed any chemicals around our garden recently. Nope, not that either. So in the end, we knew he'd reacted to something but we weren't sure what "it" was.

I held Max tightly around his midsection to keep him still while she quickly injected the medicine into a thick roll of fur at the back of his neck. The medicine would help to reduce the swelling and a follow-up course of antibiotics would have him right as rain in no time, she assured me. I gave Max his first tablet with dinner that night, and within the hour, he was fast asleep. So sleepy that he didn't get up for his midnight piddle and ended up wetting his doggie bed. A whimper woke me early in the morning, and there he was standing drowsily at the end of the bed, his head plopped on top of the doona cover. When I walked him back to his bed, I noticed that the fur on one of his back legs felt wet. Turning on the bedroom light, I saw a dark, wet section on his doggie bed. Further investigation (the good old sniff test) revealed it was urine. That was the first, but not the last, time I gave Max a bath in the wee small hours of the morning (antibiotics had that effect on him). After giving him a warm bath and towel dry, I threw the doggie bed in the laundry room and picked Max up to sleep with me on my bed. He slept soundly and without incident until the morning. By morning, his lumps had disappeared, and he seemed like his normal self. We never did find out what had caused the reaction, and there was never a repeat performance, thank goodness.

Max's curiosity didn't always lead to trouble. As a puppy, everything was new to him. Inside the house, he was especially fascinated by shoes and the sound of the toilet flushing. Outside the house, he loved to explore all areas of the backyard. One crisp autumn morning, the second day after Max joined our family, I had him out in the backyard so that he could become familiar with his surroundings. He was standing on the grass in the corner of the yard, sniffing the ground, when a gust of wind squalled through the branches of a large birch tree above him, causing the leaves to rustle and many to fall to the ground. He was so surprised to see the papery leaves floating down from above him. At first scared, he then became mesmerised every time a gust of wind blew and more leaves fell. Playing with the leaves became a great game as he used his front paws to crunch them and spread them around. The look on his face was a mix of such wonderment and curiosity, and I found myself looking forward to this morning ritual every day for the remaining days of autumn.

Sammie was also an incredibly curious dog—always poking his nose (and front paws) into anything that drew his attention. On the property in New South Wales, Sammie would often wander to the boundary. He was never away for too long, and I could see him wherever he was on the property from the windows of our house. This particular day, he came running frantically back to the house. I could tell something was clearly wrong from his panicked demeanour. He raced in through the open front door and made a beeline to where I was standing. "What's wrong mate?" I asked him, and he plopped to the floor and looked up at me with sad eyes. One of his front paws came up and brushed his nose. He seemed distressed, and when I bent down to look at his face, he nuzzled his nose into my hand and shook his head gently back and forth. As I held the weight of his head in my hand, I noticed his jowl on the right-hand side was slightly swollen. *Oh crap*, I thought, *he's been bitten by something.*

Sammie was the type of dog who totally dropped his bundle when he got sick or injured. The problem with this was that I never knew how sick he really was because even the most minor of injuries had him acting like he was at death's door. On this occasion, I was very concerned not knowing what had bitten him. Our property was in an area where the sightings of poisonous snakes and spiders were a weekly occurrence. I rang the local vet who said we'd better come in. I called Sammie out to the car, and for a dog that normally bounced onto the front seat without a second thought, he barely managed the strength to prop up on his back legs and put his front paws on the seat. I had to lift his rear end so that he could get into the car.

The trip to the vet's place was excruciating for me, as I considered all of the nasty things that could have bitten him and the potential poison pumping through his bloodstream. By the time we arrived, I was beside myself. Sammie's face was so puffy his eyes were nearly covered by his swollen jowls. His breathing was fast and shallow and his tongue lolled limply out the side of his mouth. His head hung low as he plodded from the car to the vet's office. The vet thoroughly examined him and pronounced the source of Sammie's malady as a humble, run-of-the-mill bee sting. Sammie had battled a bee and lost. Due to his jowls being so swollen, he had to stay at the vet's overnight because he couldn't eat or drink and needed to be hooked up to an intravenous drip to keep him hydrated. Twenty-four hours and $650 later, I picked up a much happier boxer. The bounce had returned to his step as had the twinkle to his eyes. He had survived his first and, thankfully, last tussle with a bee.

ANGELA LEMANIS

Sammie's sense of curiosity often made me laugh. The first time he saw himself in the full-length mirror in my bedroom was one of these times. When he encountered his reflection in the mirror, he thought it was another dog standing there looking back at him. He barked at it like, "Who are you?" And of course, his reflection barked back at him. He hunched down, bum in the air, and then bounced at the mirror. His reflection did the same. He picked up one of his front paws and pawed at the mirror, convinced that he was having a real interaction with another dog. I ushered him out of the room, but he never lost interest in this. He'd pop into the bedroom and stare at his image frequently. "You still here? Wanna play?"

Towser also found himself in the middle of a few curiosity-induced quandaries. One sunny afternoon when I was fifteen, I was home by myself with Towser. Mum and Dad had gone to pick up my brother Damian from martial arts training, but I stayed home to hang out and watch videos. Towser was lounging in the family room with me for most of the afternoon but disappeared outside for what I assumed was a piddle break. A few minutes later, there was a commotion on the back steps leading up to our veranda. I popped my head out the door in time to see Towser sprinting up the steps with a manic look in his eyes. When he saw me, he skidded to a stop at my feet, turned his gaze towards his hunched butt, and then back at me. At that moment, I saw what looked like a brown rag hanging out of his bottom. Whatever it was, it was stuck half-in, half-out, was covered in poop, and was swinging from side to side as Towser tried to shift his rear end to get a better view of the imposter.

"Calm down, boy, it's OK," I said as I manoeuvred around to get a better look. I still had no idea what it was, but I did know two things: it had to come out, and I had to touch it in order for that to happen. Given the frenzied state Towser was in, I knew I couldn't waste time getting a tissue or paper towel in order to pull it out. I put my thumb and forefinger on the item and pulled gently and slowly. It started to come out, followed by more and then some more—how long was this thing? The offending item turned out to be a piece of plastic wrap which he had swallowed and was thankfully in the stage of trying to pass. I say *thankfully* because I could only imagine what might have occurred should it have become stuck inside him.

One last gentle tug, and out it came. I have never seen such a tangible sense of relief than I did in that moment in Towser's eyes. He looked at the poopy-encased item and then at his bottom and back again. He was making doubly sure that this butt-puckering experience was over. It was, this time, but over the years Towser brought more half-in, half-out items to my attention. Mostly my brother's used hankies and dirty socks as Towser found these items far too alluring to resist. I was the only family member who ever had to rescue Towser from his backdoor hijinks. He saved these special moments purely for me.

Towser was incredibly curious when on his walks around the neighbourhood. He took the time to notice every small change—the smell of the neighbour's freshly mown lawn, the laughing cry of the Kookaburra bird as it sat perched in a nearby gum tree, or the sight of the postman delivering the mail. I'll never forget the expression on his face the first time he saw a horse. He was on one of his walks to the large reserve at the end of our street. The reserve was a vast woody area with mature trees and several ponds and walking paths. People would frequently walk their dogs there, and those with horses would often ride through on the wide walking paths as well.

One wintery afternoon, Mum and I were walking Towser when a horse and its teenage rider came trotting towards us. Towser stopped abruptly as the unfamiliar creature came into sight. His ears pricked up as did the fur on the back of his neck. His expression suggested that he was thinking, *What the hell kind of dog is that?* and he looked up at Mum and then me for reassurance. As the horse came closer, Towser backed up cautiously so that instead of his usual walking position about two feet in front of us, he was positioned directly in between Mum's legs and mine. Towser was internally debating the "fight or flight" strategy, and in the end, did neither (the good old "freeze" option). The horse nonchalantly trotted past completely unconcerned by our presence. Towser, meanwhile, was frozen to his spot in awe of the monstrous and majestic beast that had just passed by. It wasn't until the horse was a safe distance away that Towser began madly sniffing the ground where the horse had passed. If a dog could look gobsmacked, then Towser accomplished it at that moment. After giving Towser a few minutes to finish investigating the scene, we continued on. For the rest of the walk, Towser regularly looked around to make sure the horse wasn't secretly sneaking up behind him on a return visit.

Even though my dogs have found themselves in a few sticky situations from following their curiosity, the pleasurable moments exploring their territory and learning about their world prevailed.

Whenever their curiosity was piqued, they'd follow it. Sometimes they paid a price, but I get the feeling that, if they could talk, they'd attest that the positive results of exercising their curiosity still outweighed the negative.

It made me ponder the importance of adults continuing to indulge their curiosity. Curiosity and learning have been with us for all of our lives—from childhood when we were exploring the boundaries and asking "why?" to adulthood, when following one's curiosity provides inspiration, discovery, increased awareness, and further expands our knowledge base. Continuing to learn is what keeps the mind active and the soul young. By determining what we've learned about ourselves, our experiences, our passions, and our dreams, we can continue to pursue the unknown and go beyond the boundaries of familiarity. You are never too old to try something new. Curiosity may have killed the cat, but satisfaction certainly brought it back!

LESSON 13

Patience Please

WHAT DO YOU need to be a boxer owner? Plenty of patience! The boxer dog's sheer enthusiasm for life and everything in it means that they get into everything and are quite difficult to train—mainly because it takes a sturdy effort to maintain their concentration for any length of time before they get bored and want to run off and investigate the surrounding area.

Teaching Sammie to walk on a leash when he was eleven weeks old was an interesting experience. At the breeder's place, he and his sister had been allowed to run freely around in their large grassy pen, and when I took Sammie home, he had enjoyed the same freedom inside the house. He was free to investigate his surroundings and often followed me closely when I walked around the house. But when he was old enough and had received his vaccinations to protect him against parvovirus, canine distemper, infectious canine hepatitis, parainfluenza, and leptospirosis, I decided the time had come to introduce him to the big wide world outside our doorstep—but that involved training him to walk on a leash for the first time.

Attaching the leash to his tiny red collar and walking towards the door, Sammie was doing exactly as I expected; he was staying close by my feet and walking next to me. But as we went through the door and outside on to the front footpath, the problems began. Sammie headed off to the left to explore the large tree next to the footpath, and I turned right to walk down the street. It was at that point, when we both went in opposite directions, that Sammie realised he was attached to something that was pulling him in another direction and not letting him do what he wanted to do.

I had read some tips on how to train your puppy to walk on a leash, and they suggested that you should walk with your puppy and when he begins to pull, to stop immediately and call him back over to you. Under no circumstances should you keep walking when your puppy is pulling at the end of the leash. Right, good advice, but I didn't even get to the "normal walking" stage. Sammie went straight to walking at the end of the leash. When he realised that he couldn't walk any further in the direction of his wishes, he sat down and looked at me. "C'mon, Sammie, come here," I said as I bent down to coax him over towards me. He didn't budge. I got a treat out of my pocket and held it down at his level and tried to use that to tempt him over to where I was. He got up to move towards the direction of the tree again, and when the leash wouldn't let him, he decided to try and grab at the collar with his front paw. All this achieved was Sammie spinning 'round in circles and getting his paws and body entwined in the leash while he tried to tug at the collar—which had now become the sole source of his frustration. I stepped forward to untangle him and to get him to walk forward with me, but he sat down and continued his fight against the leash.

I then did the worst thing you can do when training your puppy to walk on the leash for the first time; I tugged gently at the leash to pull him my way. His tiny bottom was on the ground and his head and neck pulled back in resistance against the gentle tugs I was giving him. He wasn't going anywhere! I remember thinking to myself, *Come on, you furry nugget of obstinacy*! But he had made up his mind. He didn't like this leash thingy. Our mini tug of war continued for a few more minutes until I took a step towards him. The leash went slack, and I waited patiently to see what his next move would be. After looking at me quizzically for a few seconds, Sammie got to his feet and tentatively moved towards the same tree he'd initially wanted to investigate. I moved with him so that the leash was loose. I could see that I was going to have to be patient with Sammie until he got used to being on the leash and could see that it wasn't his enemy. I kept thinking to myself, *Sammie, one day, this leash is going to be your best friend,* but it was going to take baby steps to get to that point.

Food was a good motivator for Sammie, so I used treats often to help gain his trust in the leash. I also used dogged persistence in taking him out for walkies every day—however short they may have been in the beginning—just so he could get used to the walk and its benefits. In no time, he had the hang of it, and we then moved on to practising the "heel" command. Sammie grew to love his leash because it meant that he got to venture outside the confines of the yard each day—it became his connection to the world beyond the front gate.

Max took to the leash early and was better with it than Sammie had been initially. He didn't mind having the collar put on him, and

I introduced the leash within days of bringing him home. He was too young to go walking outside because he hadn't completed his full course of vaccinations, but I would put the leash on him, and we'd wander around the house with it on. Sometimes, I would hold the end of it in my hand; and other times, I'd let it trail across the floor behind him. When he was finally ready to go for "walkies" outside; Max and his leash were on good terms with each other.

Max's funny little quirk was that he didn't want to leave the driveway and the safety of the front yard at first. He would walk from the front door to the boundary of our property but didn't want to step out onto the footpath. Again food became a good motivator. I would coax him out with a nice piece of tasty cheese, and we would turn right at the end of the driveway, step onto the footpath, and walk further away from the house each day. Eventually, we made it to the end of the street.

On the return trips, Max would turn off into the driveway of our house automatically. One day on our return trek from the end of the street, I decided that instead of turning into our driveway, I would walk Max past it so that he could investigate the footpath that was to the left of our driveway—the other end of the street. Max didn't want a bar of it. He looked at me as if to say, "Where are you going? We missed the turn off for our house." He walked with me but kept looking back in the direction of our house, convinced that I must have made a mistake and forgotten where we lived. After we made it to the bottom of the street, which ended in a cul-de-sac, we turned around and headed home. This time, Max wasn't going to miss our driveway again. He rushed to the end of the leash and had turned into our driveway with gusto, almost yanking my arm out of its socket, until I could bring him back to "heel" again. When we got to the front door, he seemed very pleased with himself for showing me the way home.

In what can often be an impatient world, my boxers have been the ones to teach me that good things come to those who wait. Instead of my dogs learning new skills on my timetable, they reminded me that everyone—including dogs—learns things at their own pace. Knowledge can't be forced or rushed. We all learn when we are ready to, and patience is important if we are to successfully understand and retain new information.

One of my favourite memories of patience personified was when Towser and I played a game which consisted of fridge magnets being thrown at the fridge while he tried to catch them midflight. It was one of his favourite games. I'd use several large flat magnets and would sit on the kitchen floor about a metre from the fridge door and throw the magnets one by one at the fridge. Sitting patiently beside me, Towser would wait for just the right moment before trying to grab the magnet as it flew through the air and before it stuck to the fridge door. Towser would sit so still, every muscle fibre tense, his eyes focused intently on the movement of my hand so that he could anticipate the perfect time to lunge and grab the magnet as it sailed through the air. Most times, he got it right and caught the magnet midflight, but if he was too slow, it would stick to the fridge right in front of his eyes. He always seemed surprised when it stuck and looked at me with such wonder in his eyes as if he were asking, "How does it do that?"

I'd peel the magnet off the fridge, and he would come back beside me and wait patiently until I threw it again. If I didn't throw them at just the right angle so the magnetic backing hit the fridge door flatly, the magnets would bounce off the fridge and land on the kitchen floor. At that point, Towser would pounce on them, bring them back, and drop them into my outstretched hand. Towser was always so pleased with himself when he caught the magnets in mid-air, and he never got bored with the game. Often, he would be the one prompting us to play. I'd find him in the kitchen standing next to the fridge ready to go.

Sammie also showed the ultimate in patience when trying to catch flies in the kitchen. Living in the sunny tropics, the doors and windows of our house were often open in order to let the cool breeze circulate through the place. Even though every window and door had screens on it, there always seemed to be a couple of flies that made it through when a door was opened. Sammie for some reason decided that fly catching was going to be his sport of choice.

Upon spotting a fly, he would go into stalking mode and try to sneak up on it. When the fly took flight, Sammie's ears would pop up and his head would snap around trying to keep track of where it went. He would be so engrossed in finding and following the fly, he often didn't know I was even there watching him until I'd say, "Where's the fly? Go get the fly." He'd bounce around, pop up onto his hind legs or sneak across the floor in a delicate tiptoe fashion—whatever was required at that point in the hunt. Most times, he was too slow, but every now and then he got one. His mouth would snap open and shut, and he seemed surprised himself to have finally caught the much sought after bounty. A few seconds later, the

ANGELA LEMANIS

slobber-covered fly would be unceremoniously spat back onto the floor. The thrill for Sammie was in the hunt, but he had no idea what to do with the fly once he'd captured it. Still, it was an exercise in patience and seemed to fulfil some basic predatory instinct.

Dogs can have amazing levels of patience, and they use this patience to finish what they start. In all of the above examples, my dogs never contemplated that they wouldn't achieve what they'd set out to do.

The word *patience* comes from the Latin word *patientia*, which means "to suffer with fortitude; to bear, to endure hardship, difficulty, or inconvenience without complaint, to have self-control, and to willingly tolerate." Patience is the ability to deal with a delay without becoming irritated or annoyed by it.

Want to practise patience? Train a puppy. You certainly need plenty of tolerance and a cool head for that. It takes adequate time, a resilient mind, a gentle voice, an assured demeanour, and plenty of staying power to get your puppy or dog's attention and keep it long enough to train your pet. Time and patience are key because you should never be rushed when trying to teach your pup new things. They will sense it if you are getting frustrated because you don't have enough time to spend with them. Don't have unrealistic expectations either—they are young, and you are asking them to concentrate purely on you and the task at hand. They haven't had to do that before so you need to be gentle with them and understand they are little and will get tired quickly.

I'm always in awe of how puppies learn new skills—we are speaking a foreign language to them often in high-pitched tones and with animated hand gestures, and they seem to decipher exactly what we are asking of them in a relatively quick amount of time. We might arrange them in the correct sitting position and say "sit". In the space of a few hours a puppy can make the link between the word and the action. If only I could learn other languages as quickly and easily.

Max learned lots of skills one-on-one with me when he was very little. He picked up the sit, down, stay, come, and no bark skills very quickly. From the first night I had him, he began to understand the word *piddles*. I took him outside each evening before bed and said "piddles," and when he did piddle (sometimes after a period of wandering around sniffing grass and looking out through the gate), I would reward him and make a fuss. After a week of doing this, I could let him out and say the word, and he would piddle straight away. We have done this every night since and continue to do it still.

The only trouble I had with Max not paying attention to me was at dog obedience training when he was surrounded by plenty of other dogs. While obedient inside the yard, the distractions outside the yard proved too intriguing to ignore. Max had attended a four-week puppy socialisation course when he was twelve weeks old, which was followed by another four-week dog obedience course. While doing well at both of these courses, he still had trouble paying attention to me when we were out in public and there were other dogs around. He was always far too interested in what they were doing to listen to the commands I was giving him. I thought another more intensive stint of dog obedience training was in order to make sure he listened to me when there were multiple distractions around him. So I enrolled him for an eight-week dog obedience course, and every Tuesday night, we'd say good-bye to Andrej, jump in the car, and go to our lesson.

There were all sorts of dogs at the obedience training school: an elegant miniature schnauzer, a very regal cavalier King Charles spaniel, two feisty Jack Russell terriers, an incredibly fluffy bichon frise, a few other spirited boxers, a well-behaved pit bull terrier, a rather aloof Alaskan malamute, several golden retrievers and yellow labradors, and a massively built but beautifully mellow bull mastiff. All in all, a good representation from the doggie kingdom. Max took part in the introductory sniffing session that began every class as they all acquainted themselves with each other again.

The instructor then got us all to line our dogs up and commanded us to get our dogs to sit and stay. We then walked our dogs around in a circle while asking them to "look at me" when we wanted to gain their attention. We'd then get our dogs to lie down and stay while the owners walked away from them. If they stayed in place until we returned, each dog got a treat. Max fared well with each skill, but about halfway through the hour-long class, Max became bored. He'd had enough of constantly paying attention to me and sitting, staying, and walking. He'd had enough of the treats I'd given him and wasn't responding to his squeaky toy or any other attention-getting method. It was as if he'd checked out. He'd decided he'd had enough of the learning for that evening and was actively searching the park to see what else was going on that he could partake in. It was at that exact point that the instructor made the decision to try a new skill—one where the owner got their dog to sit and stay while the owner dropped the leash and walked about one hundred metres away. The ideal outcome was for the dog to stay obediently where he or she was until the owner called or whistled, at which point the dog could go racing towards their owner. I knew Max was getting antsy and distracted, so it was with great trepidation that I participated in this exercise.

I looked at Max and said assertively, "Sit," to which he sat and then "stay." He focused on me as I put the end of his leash on the ground and held my hand up as a signal for him to continue to stay where he was while I began to walk backwards away from his position. So far, so good. Twenty-five metres, still good. Fifty metres and holding. Seventy-five metres and still paying attention. One hundred metres. Yes, success! He was still there, looking at me and waiting.

The instructor said, "OK, call your dogs." And I yelled, "C'mon, Max, come." He took off and was heading straight for me—*phew, this was working perfectly* I thought to myself—until he looked across to his left and started to veer off course towards the fluffy bichon frise. *Oh no, this isn't good*, I thought as visions of Max crash tackling the tiny white dog came to mind. But Max kept running, past the startled bichon frise and one of the interested yellow labs and straight towards the fence line of the park where he came to an abrupt stop and began sniffing the grass before squatting for a piddle. I had taken off after him while all of the other owners had their dogs coming to them as was required from the exercise.

When I got close enough to grab the end of Max's leash, he looked at me as if he didn't know why I was frazzled and out of breath. Securing his leash in my hand, I walked with him back to the instructor and told her I was taking him home. He'd clearly had enough for one night, and she agreed. He slept soundly on the back seat the entire drive home. We did go back and complete the course, and as the weeks went by, Max's attention span improved, but it took plenty of patience on both our parts for the achievement to be realised.

Exercising patience on a regular basis is a worthy endeavour. When a state of patience is achieved, it brings happiness and a release from the feelings of frustration, irritation, anxiousness, stress, or anger that a person who is lacking in patience feels when faced with a tough situation. Again, it comes back to what you can and can't control. For me, patience has been a difficult skill to master. Sometimes the slightest thing—a traffic jam, no mobile phone reception, buses that don't run on time, instruction manuals that sprout absolute gibberish—is enough to send my temper from zero to ten as my internal rage thermostat goes KA BOOM, KA PLOW. The following story was one scenario that made me stop and think about my reactions to life's little challenges.

One morning, I found myself standing in line at the post office, and an old lady was up the front conducting a lengthy conversation with the post office clerk about the weather and the price of stamps, while all I needed was one single solitary stamp. I could feel the irritation beginning as I started to get frustrated with the delay. The frustration then turned into a simmering annoyance, which then gave way to total infuriation. An angry voice inside my head said, "Why can't the old lady just get on with purchasing the stuff she needs—forget the conversation. Doesn't she realise there is a queue of people behind her who, quite frankly, don't give a rats about the price of stamps! And what about the post office clerk? Why doesn't she cut the conversation short and politely move the old lady on so that she can serve us. Remember service? Of course, this was all my internal dialogue as I would never consider saying anything out loud or do anything that would create a scene. I just quietly simmered away until I got my stamp and left the scene that had caused me such angst. Or should I say, the scene that I had allowed to cause me such angst.

Reviewing this situation later—when I had calmed down and could consider the situation with a clearer perspective and the wisdom of hindsight—I was uncomfortable with how I had let myself become so wound up by something so minor. I hypothesised that maybe the old lady's outing to the post office that day and the conversation with the clerk might have been one of a few social interactions she might have had that day. Maybe she is a widow and going out to do errands once a week is as much of a social outing as it is about doing the errands. Maybe she's lonely.

Instead of getting cranky, I could have removed myself from the situation and gone back to the post office at another time. Or maybe I could have just taken a few deep breaths and waited patiently without getting frustrated about it. The old lady wasn't deliberately having a lengthy conversation just to make me frustrated or to spite me. She was probably not aware that there was such a queue behind her. The post office clerk might not have known how to end the conversation quickly without seeming rude. The bigger picture is that none of this was done on purpose or with malicious intent. It was just what happened at that point on that day.

With impatience, irritation, and anger, the only person you are doing a disservice to is yourself. You get all worked up for no point—getting infuriated and annoyed is not going to make the queue move any faster. This is just what happens in life sometimes. Life is messy. There are approximately seven billion people inhabiting this world, and we all have our own agenda and schedules. We all want to get on with our day according to our timeframe. Well, folks, it just doesn't work in our favour all of the time.

Impatience or anger is never the best answer to a situation. If you do have an outburst and complain, most times you end up feeling crappy about it later. Crappy that you let yourself get that angry and disappointed that you lost control. Impatience is also unhealthy for the mind and body. It leads to anxiety, raises your blood pressure, can induce headaches, sends your adrenal glands into overdrive and floods the body with stress hormones such as adrenaline and cortisol. These hormones over time can cause numerous health effects like depression, heart attack, and stroke because the body isn't supposed to be inundated with these chemicals on a regular basis.

I'm sure we are all familiar with these moments of impatience that lead to insidious frustration—like when the computer crashes in the middle of an important document; when someone steals the parking spot that you have been, until then, patiently waiting for; when someone puts an empty milk carton back into the fridge; when the printer keeps jamming; or when the person at the grocery store leaves the trolley in the centre of the aisle so that you can't get past. There are so many occasions during the day and so many interactions with other people that can test our patience levels. I now know that the only thing I can control is how I will react to each situation. Patience can be very hard to practise, but it is a skill that can be developed, and it can become your best asset—it is a virtue after all!

Dogs know that everything gets accomplished in its own good time. There's a saying that "the trees that are the slowest to grow bear the most fruit," which goes to show that sometimes you can't rush a good thing. It's worth the wait, and patience is a very necessary quality for an evolved human to have.

Make Sure You Always Know the Way Home

HAVING A CLEAR direction in life is a wonderful thing. To know where we are headed is good for our overall well-being and sense of purpose for the future. Having goals helps us to determine what we want out of life, the direction we'd like to take in certain areas of our lives (such as career, personal development, or education) and channels our attention to the achievements we'd like to have in our future. But focusing solely on the future is problematic if we can't or won't also quietly reflect on our past.

Like everything in nature, there needs to be balance. Knowing where you're going means being mindful of where you've been. It's similar to the traditional Chinese concept of yin-yang balance, where yin and yang exist harmoniously alongside each other. Our past and future are similar in theory: our future cannot exist without our past, and our past is only our past because there's a future. We have to understand our past to understand the future. In a world of balance, one cannot exist without the other.

No matter how far we go in life and how far we spread our wings, or how many achievements and successes we've had, I believe it's important to remember where we've come from and to be appreciative of that.

The best way for me to ground myself when life accelerates too quickly is to go back to my parents' place—a place that always makes me feel immediately at home. My parents have lived in the same house for twenty-five years, and my brother owns a house in the same neighbourhood. It's almost like stepping back in time because my parents' home is a place that holds special memories of many happy times spent with Mum, Dad, Damian, Towser, and Sammie. It's a welcoming safe haven where I feel looked after—my mum still cooks for me when I'm there even though I don't expect her to, and my parents still have their same routine that they've followed for years: dinner out on Friday night and Sunday morning breakfast down by the beach. Going home to visit as an adult, I get to sleep in my old room, and I get to drive their car. It's wonderful—I'm on holiday but surrounded with a familiar setting and the people I love.

Home is a significant place—it's where your foundation was established, where your roots took hold, and where your moral compass was set. Where we've come from has helped to mould us into the people we are today—the experiences we've had, the people we've known, the people who've loved us, along with the choices we've made, have all shaped our lives into what they are in this current moment.

Thomas Wolfe wrote in his posthumously published 1940 novel, *You Can't Go Home Again*, that the passage of time meant one couldn't go back because "back" had changed and was no longer the same place you had experienced before.

He wrote, "You can't go back home to your family, back home to your childhood . . . back home to a young man's dreams of glory and of fame . . . to singing just for singing's sake . . . away from all the strife and conflict of the world . . . back home to someone who can help you, save you, ease the burden for you, back home to the old forms and systems of things which once seemed everlasting but which are changing all the time—back home to the escapes of Time and Memory."

My belief is that if home was a happy place then you can, and should, go home again but only for short periods of time. As with any visiting guest, grown kids can overstay their welcome if not careful. Just because you feel comfortable going back home doesn't necessarily mean that your parents' want you back indefinitely. When your parents say, "You always have a home to come back to," they should also add the caveat, "if you call in advance and we can set some boundaries, like when you're going to leave again." My mum would probably disagree with this (I can hear her saying, "You are always welcome here"), but my dad is probably nodding his head regarding the boundary issue! And parents setting boundaries with their adult children is not a bad thing. Having an understanding with your parents about what is acceptable in an adult relationship is necessary for both parties. Being considerate of your parents' space helps to keep the relationship healthy because no one feels like they are being taken for granted.

While I enjoyed a great relationship with my parents when I was a child and a teenager, I have an incredible relationship with them as an adult. The pressure is off them now as they have already raised me, and I have become an independent, successful, happy person in my own right. They raised me well and sent me out into the world so their "job" in the traditional parenting role is complete. Now I consider them my friends, my confidantes, my advisors. They've lived more life than me, and I can now appreciate that their views, advice, and words of wisdom are based on having had more life experiences, and not simply to put a dent in my enthusiasm (as I sometimes thought as a "spirited" teenager). We don't always want to hear these views when we are teenagers as most times we think we know better and believe that we are 100 percent bulletproof. But once you've lived some life as an adult—and especially those who have had children of their own—you realise that your parents were not just telling you stuff to "control your life" (dramatic pause) but because they just knew more than you did.

I get nostalgic when I stay at my parents' place. I fondly remember Towser sitting with me out in the backyard or Sammie sleeping on the ground outside my bedroom window when I was home visiting. I know where, and under which tree, Towser's ashes are buried in the garden and where Sammie's urn is. Towser and Sammie's presence is still palpable around the place and especially when I walk down the hallway from the dining room to the kitchen—I half expect two little tan boxer heads to pop around the corner and greet me. I like feeling that they are there. It reminds me of how much I loved them both and how they brought so much joy to me and everyone who came into that house. Even the discreet section of lawn on the far side of the yard where they went to do their "business" hasn't fully recovered after many years of use. The grass grows, but it has a different look to the rest of the lawn. My parents' home just holds all of the wonderful memories of my family and exudes the love we've all shared over the course of many years.

Even the city where my parents' live, Townsville, is special to me. To me it's my hometown—it's where most of my relatives still live, it has some of my favourite places to go, and it's where I remember my grandparents. I like going shopping or for a walk along the beach and bumping into people I've known for years. I like knowing that people knew my grandparents and, similarly, know my parents. I like knowing most of the street and road names, and I like how familiar it all feels to me when I'm there. I mean what's not to like? Townsville is a beautiful coastal city that boasts palm trees, blue water, golden sandy beaches, warm sunny weather most of the year, and picturesque islands—namely Magnetic Island, which is situated in the waters of the World Heritage listed Great Barrier Reef Marine Park. The city has been changing and progressing over the last decade or so, which is true of most places, but a good percentage of it is still the same.

It's also one of those small cities that people leave but often come back to because the lifestyle is just so relaxed.

If, however, "home" was a source of sorrow, distress, or trouble, then maybe you shouldn't go home again. I am not naive enough to think that everybody enjoyed a happy, loving home life. For some, Wolfe's statement that you can't go home again might be more aptly stated, "You wouldn't ever want to go home again." For some, their childhood might have been more reminiscent of a series of unfortunate events that they managed to grow up and escape from. For some, the unfortunate events might have started after leaving the safety and security of the childhood home. Whatever the situation, we've all had some stumbles on our journey of "growing up."

Sometimes, we find that our ambition and our goal setting, whilst good at first, takes us away from where we really want to be. Concentrating solely on setting and achieving goals, without proper consideration and regular reflection of whether those goals still serve our purpose and whether their achievement will add to our life journey, can have a negative outcome.

I remember vividly a conversation I had with a gentleman I knew who remarked exhaustedly, "I feel completely lost at the moment." He was talking about his life in general, and it reminded me of a few conversations I've had with some of my closest friends. A couple of close friends spoke of how they'd achieved everything that was expected of them and realised goals that they thought they wanted in their twenties, only to find themselves questioning the decisions they'd made. Their comments were regarding their careers. They'd received good marks in high school, went to university and completed degrees and postgraduate studies, interviewed, and became employed by high-profile multinational corporations and had excelled at every stage. Now in their mid to late thirties, they were reassessing whether they even actually liked their career choice. They were feeling lost because everything they had worked so hard for, and received so much recognition for, was actually making them unhappy. Their goals and ambitions had changed—what was important to them now had changed. Work and career weren't the be-all and end-all anymore. Now instead of high-powered careers, they wanted worthwhile, meaningful, well-rounded lives. They had set so many goals that were focused predominantly on their careers that they had forgotten to reassess as they got older and their personal aspirations changed.

There's no doubt that life can take us in unexpected directions, and we can oftentimes find ourselves walking paths we didn't necessarily plan.

ANGELA LEMANIS

If someone had said to me fifteen years ago that I would be living in New Zealand and writing a book, I would have chuckled. But we never really know what's on the path ahead for us—what twists and turns our journey will take. We will find ourselves reassessing decisions and beliefs that once held true but might not anymore, or making choices that once would never have appealed. That's the beauty of life and change.

It's when it gets to this point, where you are questioning certain aspects of your life, that family and friends sustain us. They help us when we get lost. One of my friends provided encouraging words that came originally from a Nemo Nox quote, "When there are rocks in your path, keep them all. With them you shall build your castle." And I have been collecting the rocks along the way, taking note of which of my decisions created the issue and making sure I took some learning from it. One of those learnings is that to get where you want to go, you have to know where you've been.

Even Max demonstrated the importance of knowing the way back home. Max loved to run off-leash. As soon as the leash was unclipped, Max would tremble with anticipation waiting for Andrej to say it's OK for him to go. Literally within one one-hundredth of a second of the word leaving Andrej's lips, Max would be off, running at full tilt, tongue out, head bobbing up and down as his legs quickly stretched to capacity, touched the ground, and retracted again. It was poetry in motion. He looked so happy and free as he sprinted from side to side across the width of the park. After about five minutes, he'd come back and start sniffing the trees or the ground before taking off again in another burst of energy. Andrej enjoyed seeing Max like this and would often take him off the leash in the parks surrounding our street—even though he knew I was uncomfortable with it. My biggest fear was that Max would spot something that piqued his interest, and he would take off to investigate without thinking about it. My biggest fear was that he wouldn't come back.

One crisp spring morning, my biggest fear came true. Andrej was up at the crack of dawn and decided to take Max out for his walk a little earlier than was usual. The sound of Max bouncing around in the kitchen, waiting for Andrej to attach the leash, woke me out of a sound sleep. I heard them leave through the back gate before proceeding to fall back to sleep again.

Andrej and Max headed down to the park, and once there and realising they had the park to themselves, Andrej took Max off the leash so that he could run out his energy. Max complied and galloped enthusiastically across the park; his warm breath coming out in little white puffs in the chilly morning air. When Max ran out of *oomph*, he fell in beside Andrej, and together they walked down one of the park's tree-lined walking paths. Max was behaving himself, casually sniffing the shrubbery and other low-lying vegetation, so instead of putting him back on the leash (as Andrej would normally have done), he let Max roam free for a little while longer.

Engrossed in investigating the sniffs and scents of the park at dawn, Max didn't see or hear a fast-moving cyclist approach from behind until the cyclist was passing by. Noticing the sudden movement beside him, Max became spooked and immediately bolted in the opposite direction away from the cyclist, completely ignoring Andrej's calls to come back. Andrej knew he was in trouble when Max's little brown body disappeared over the hill and out of sight.

Oh crap, Andrej thought as he broke into a run in the direction that Max had just disappeared from. Cresting over the small hill, Andrej searched the landscape for signs of Max, but he was nowhere to be seen. With a rising sense of dread, Andrej repeatedly called Max's name in the hope that he would suddenly appear out of the nearby shrubbery or from behind a tree.

"Max, come here boy," Andrej called. Nothing. No movement, no Max. Andrej started searching throughout the park, continuing to call Max's name and whistling every few seconds. A sick feeling rose from the pit of Andrej's stomach as the realisation that Max could be anywhere and might be lost entered Andrej's mind for the first time. After half an hour of searching, whistling, and calling, Andrej knew he had to return home and leave a message with the local council to advise them of a lost dog should they get any calls from concerned residents reporting a wayward boxer. Another nauseating thought dawned on Andrej—he would have to tell me that Max was missing. Knowing that I never felt secure with him taking Max off-leash because of the boxer's unpredictability when allowed to roam freely (which was always my experience with Towser and Sammie), he knew I wouldn't take the news well.

I all too clearly recall the time I had to chase and crash tackle Towser because he managed to escape the confines of the backyard, and was running around the neighbourhood and wouldn't come back when called. Towser's escapade had been in Townsville when he managed to get out through the back gate. He bolted off and ran in a bizarre zigzag-darting motion. He then turned abruptly and pounded back towards where I was standing, frantically waving my arms and yelling his name. He raced to within a metre of my position and then proceeded straight past me. To

ANGELA LEMANIS

him, it was a great game. I would lunge to grab him and he would go sprinting right on by.

On his next trip towards me, I got down low and committed to tackling Towser when he got to within tackling distance. Towser was gunning straight for me, and I took a deep breath, waited until he was about a metre from me, and then dove right on top of him. He collapsed to the ground with me on top, and I grabbed his collar and got both of us back on our feet. I was mad but incredibly relieved to be able to walk Towser back to the yard and secure him safely behind the gate.

Andrej was not as lucky. He couldn't see Max anywhere so he made for home. By the time he got back on our street, his mind had listed all of the potential scenarios that Max could be facing at that moment. Was he hiding alone somewhere scared or running frantically along the roads in our area? Max had no road sense whatsoever, and we have quite a few busy roads in our suburb—Andrej was hoping that Max wouldn't try to cross any.

Rounding the corner of the front fence and entering the yard, Andrej saw the best sight he could have wished for. Max was standing in the front yard looking forlorn and scared. Upon seeing Andrej, Max's expression turned to pure happiness and he jelly bean danced his way towards his walking buddy. Luckily, Max had known his way home after the fright he got from the man on the bicycle. Andrej wasted no time securing Max in the safety of the backyard and Max, tired from the morning's activities, promptly drifted off to sleep.

It took Andrej a couple of days to tell me what had happened that morning. He knew I would be freaked out that we had nearly lost Max but in truth, I think it took him a couple of days to get over the shock of it too. I'm just so thankful that Max knew the way home.

It's an old cliché, but "home is where the heart is." And it's a cliché because even though it is a well-worn term that has been overly used and abused, it has truth. I am lucky to have two places where I feel at home. One is the house I share with Andrej and Max, and the other is my parents' house. Both places make me feel warm, safe, and secure. In both places I am surrounded by the people and belongings that I love and treasure. As Henry Van Dyke said of home, and I wholeheartedly concur:

Every house where love abides
And friendship is a guest,
Is surely home, and home sweet home

For there the heart can rest.

My wish is that everyone can have this type of refuge to return to—and every boxer dog too of course—and that no matter where we are headed in life, we always know how to get home to the ones who love us most.

ANGELA LEMANIS

LESSON 15

Good-bye Just Might Be the Saddest Word

LEARNING TO LET go is possibly the hardest life lesson. I know that loved ones will always be with you because you keep them alive in your heart and mind, but the actual moment of letting go and saying good-bye is heart-wrenchingly hard.

It took me a long time to get over the deaths of Towser and Sammie. I had always prepared myself, but I wasn't quite ready for their final days.

Towser was ten and a half years of age and enjoying his twilight years. He'd spend the day lazing in the sun, sleeping on his dog bed on the veranda, or lounging on the cool tile hallway in my parents' house. Dad was working from home in those days so Towser had constant companionship. He would sleep on the carpet in Dad's home office for hours while Dad busily worked away on the computer. Mum would come home from work and take Towser for a short walk around the neighbourhood. Towser's hips had been a problem for a while, and he could only manage the shorter walks, but he loved these outings nonetheless. My parents fed Towser at the same time every night, and after eating, he would always disappear into the backyard to do his business. After about fifteen minutes, he'd wander back to the front door and tap it with his front paw, and either Mum or Dad would let him in. He'd then be settled for the night.

This particular night, everything seemed normal. He ate his meal and disappeared to the backyard. Mum and Dad were watching television when Mum noticed that Towser hadn't come knocking. Concerned that he was taking longer than usual, Mum went to see what could be keeping him. Towser was standing uncomfortably in a dark corner of the backyard, his stomach bloated and distended. As Mum got closer, he went to move and let out a low groan. Knowing that something was wrong, she immediately got Dad to ring the afterhours vet.

When my parents alerted the on-call vet that Towser's stomach was swollen and he seemed distressed, the vet was on another emergency call out with a cat that was having trouble delivering kittens. He said he was almost done and would be with my parents as soon as he could. Thirty minutes later, my parents were at the vet's clinic and being told that Towser had a twisted stomach, a condition which affects larger dog breeds that have deep, barrel chests. Boxers are one such breed.

The condition starts as a bloat when excess gas is produced as food breaks down. The stomach starts to swell and then turns around on its axis. As the stomach continues to expand, the gas and partly digested food become trapped by the twisted area. Unless something is done quickly, death will rapidly follow as the stomach swells to a very large size.

The vet moved quickly, but the only option for Towser was emergency stomach surgery—an incredibly invasive procedure to correct the stomach position and attach it in place. But there were no guarantees that, even after surgery, the stomach wouldn't twist again. Given his age and the toll the surgery and recovery would take on him, my parents decided that the most humane thing to do was not to subject Towser to such a big ordeal. The vet agreed that euthanizing him was the best decision taking everything into account, and left Mum and Dad to have some quiet time alone with Towser while he made preparations. In the space of a few hours, Towser had gone from looking forward to his dinner to just plain "gone." Mum and Dad stayed with Towser for the whole thing to provide him comfort right until the end. As traumatic as the night had been for my parents, Towser slipped peacefully away while the two people he loved with his whole heart, and who loved him just as much, stood by his side patting his head.

My parents called me that night to let me know what had happened. I was shocked and saddened that Towser was gone. It was all so sudden. I really felt for my parents as I could hear the emotion in their voices. I drove past their place later that night to see if they were awake. I wanted to go and give them a big hug and to let them know that I was feeling very sorry for them (and myself), but the house was dark. My parents, drained by the night's events, had gone to bed. Mum told me later that she and Dad didn't sleep that night so saddened were they by Towser's departure.

Sammie was three years old when Towser passed. I would find myself looking at Sammie in the wake of what had just happened to Towser, thinking, *I don't think I'll ever be ready to deal with that.* I just hoped that Sammie's time was many, many years away and that he wouldn't be in any pain when it eventually happened. His time did eventually come in 2006

ANGELA LEMANIS

when he was thirteen and a half years old. Up until March of that year, Sammie had been in good health (for an older dog that is). His arthritis was there, but it didn't prevent him from getting around or doing what he liked to do. At the beginning of May, his hips started to give him more problems. The arthritis was slowly making it harder for him to get up and down from the floor—from lying to standing position and vice versa. He seemed to be coping with it, but my parents noticed that it was becoming more and more difficult for him as he got older and weaker. At around the same time, Sammie started to have dizzy spells where he would be standing and his legs would start to wobble. By the beginning of June, things had worsened. His dizzy spells occurred more frequently, and my parents were concerned that with his bad hips, his legs might give out on him completely during a spell, and he would hurt himself. It was time to visit the vet.

The vet had seen Sammie in March that year and said that despite the arthritis, he was doing well for his age. After hearing my parents describe the dizzy spells, he ran a range of tests. Sammie had developed a cardiac arrhythmia, leaving him with an erratic heartbeat. It's considered a serious condition because if left untreated and the irregular beats occur in sequence, it can lead to collapses or sudden death.

The vet was amazed at how quickly Sammie had gone downhill since seeing him in March and determined that the best course of action at this stage, given his age and the fact that his quality of life was decreasing rapidly, was to consider doing the thing that my parents had thought but didn't want to say out loud—euthanasia. If the arrhythmia had developed when Sammie was younger, he could have had surgery to fit a pacemaker. Surgery was out of the question now because it was just too invasive for a dog his age. Given that Sammie was my dog, my parents said they wanted to talk to me before progressing.

Mum called me immediately with the news. I knew this day would come as all dog owners do, but as much as I thought I'd prepared myself, I was still overwhelmed by the finality of it all. I, like my parents, did not want Sammie to suffer in any way. He was such a beautiful dog that he deserved to be treated with the dignity and respect he deserved. There was no way of getting around it—his heart wasn't working properly. I didn't want things to get worse or to have him suffer needlessly simply because I was too scared to let him go. I had to think of him and what was best for him even though I didn't know if I could actually say the words. But I did; it was time.

Mum rang the vet on the Friday morning and made an appointment for the following Monday morning. The weekend would give them some quality time with Sammie in order to say their good-byes. Both of my parents stayed close by his side all weekend.

I had said my good-bye the last time I visited my parents the previous Christmas. Sammie and I had a great time together. Both he and I loved Christmas—he liked playing with the discarded Christmas wrapping paper, and I loved being around my family again. We played ball together, went for walks, sat together on the floor, and wrestled (gently) in the yard. I took plenty of photos of my beloved pet and gave him lots of hugs. When the holiday was over and it came time for me to leave for the airport, I knew it might be the last time I saw him. I got down on one knee so that I was at eye level with him, and I told him that I didn't know when I'd next be able to visit him. I told him that even though I wasn't there with him every day, he was always in my thoughts. I had photos of him up in my apartment everywhere, and I'd look at his cute little wrinkled face every morning and smile. I told him that he was my beautiful dog, a true friend that I loved with all my heart. Then I secretly prayed that he would be there the next time I visited so that I got to see him again. Unfortunately with that one dreaded phone call from my parents, I knew that wasn't going to be the case.

Monday morning, June 26, 2006, at 11:30 am was D-Day time. That morning, Mum sat beside him on his dog bed reading the paper. She wanted him to be where he was comfortable, but she didn't want him to be alone so she sat on the end of his dog bed with him and read the paper while he dozed. She knew that with each tick of the clock, she was drawing nearer to having to say good-bye to her buddy.

At 11:15 am, they grabbed his leash, clipped it to his collar, and walked him out to the car. At first, he thought he was going for a walk and was enthusiastically surging at the end of the leash, in a rare but always committed display of liveliness. Then he saw the open car door and his focus switched to his second favourite type of outing—the car ride. Sammie always loved his car rides, and that day was no different. He didn't know that it would be his last. He sat on the back seat, staring out the window, drool dripping off his jowls in long glistening streams. It wasn't unlike a car ride he'd taken with me a few years earlier when his constant drooling had made such a mess of my car.

It was a hot, sunny day in Townsville, and I had just finished university and purchased my first brand new car, straight off the dealership's showroom floor. It was a shiny white Honda Civic with dark grey interior. Everything on it was brand spanking new and perfect—which was a far cry from the clapped out old Datsun I'd been driving while at university. I was so proud of my new car that I treated it with kid gloves. I washed it every weekend and waxed it, vacuumed the upholstery, and polished the inside. No one was allowed to eat, drink, or smoke in my car under any conditions.

Sammie hadn't been for a ride in it yet, but on this warm, sunny day, I decided we could go for a drive down to the beach for a walk in the sea breeze. Knowing that Sammie was a terrible drooler (we used to call him slobber dog), I carefully and painstakingly placed blankets over the back seat so that the upholstery was protected.

Sammie was ready to go the moment I put him on his leash and led him out to the car. Opening the back door, Sammie leapt on to the back seat and began sniffing the new car smell. I shut the door behind him and walked around to the driver's seat.

"Sit, Sammie," I told him, but he completely ignored me and kept investigating the new surroundings. "Sit down," I said with more authority. Eventually after turning around and around, he complied. I partially lowered the back windows so that he could stick his nose out into the fresh air but also had the air-conditioning on to keep things cool. Before I had even pulled out of the driveway, the two previously spotless back windows were smeared with saliva and wet nose marks. The excitement of a car ride had sent his salivary glands into overdrive, and by the time we reached the halfway point of our drive, saliva was dribbling off his jowls in long, slimy strands and sticking to the nearest part of the car it could find.

Saliva was stuck to the headrest of the seat in front, the windows, the back doors, and the centre console area. As I quietly cringed at the unwelcome christening my car was getting, I reassured myself that at least the blankets were collecting most of it. Reassurance was useless. At that very moment, Sammie shook his head. As if in slow motion, I watched his jowls go up and down, spraying drool in every direction. "Nooooo," I cried as some of it landed on my face, but it was no use, he was in full-blown shaking mode. Nearly every inch of the inside of my car was hit—the interior roof, dashboard, gear stick, steering wheel, and me. I glanced back at him in the rear-view mirror with a look that could wither a plant only to see him, eyes bright, ears alert enjoying every minute of his outing. I couldn't stay mad at him—this was just par for the course with our slobber dog. We made it to the beach and had a fabulous time. I then spent the rest of the afternoon restoring my car to its previously clean glory.

To Sammie, the car ride to the vet that morning was no different—he was having fun—but to Mum and Dad, it marked the start of a very sad day. At the vet's place, both Mum and Dad were with Sammie, touching him when he breathed his final breath. It all happened so quickly at the end. Sammie was lying comfortably on the table, and the vet gave him a sedative prior to the euthanasia drug, so that he was restful. The euthanasia drug was then administered and Sammie's muscles relaxed and his breathing slowed, and then stopped. Sammie was in the company of friends when he passed—my parents were touching him and the vet gave him a pat as well. As difficult as it was for my parents to see their beloved pet go, they wouldn't have ever considered not being with him. It was important to them that Sammie knew they were there with him right by his side so that he wasn't scared or uncomfortable. My parents stayed for a while afterwards for their final good-byes as well. It was a peaceful ending for Sammie by all accounts.

Mum and Dad couldn't go directly home afterwards though, as the sight of his belongings—his bed, water and food bowls, and toys were there as reminders of what had just happened. As time went by, the reminders of him were slowly removed, but every now and then, a stray piece of fur would be on one of their clothes or the top of a chewed sprinkler head would remind them of him.

Meanwhile in New Zealand, I remember that fateful Monday. Andrej dropped me off at an intersection outside of my work building, and I felt a weird out-of-body sensation as I stood on the footpath waiting for the light to change so that I could cross. I felt crushed inside. I thought, *How am I going to get through today?* Sammie was booked into the vet at 11:30 am (Australian EST), which was 1:30 pm New Zealand time. I was in a meeting at 1:30 pm, and I sat looking at the clock on the wall, with the minute hand ticking away. I felt as if I were watching my little dog's life tick away. By 1:45 pm, I thought, *My beautiful dog will be gone now*, and I had to leave the meeting to go to the bathroom because the emotion was too overwhelming. My best buddy was gone. No one at work knew what was happening to my dog, and I didn't say anything either—this was private and personal to me. I felt awful I couldn't be there with him in his last moments. I had hoped he wasn't scared. I had hoped he knew how much I loved him and appreciated him. I was so worried about him. Would he be OK in the next life? When he passed and "saw the light," who would be calling his name so that he knew where to go? Who would be there to meet him at the other end? I reassured myself that maybe Towser would be waiting for him.

ANGELA LEMANIS

I cried for a week straight; I was so distraught. My parents sent me Sammie's collar, and I wrapped it carefully in some material and placed it the drawer of my bedside table (where I still keep it to this day). It smelt of him and when I found the going especially difficult, I would hold it up to my nose and smell the furry dog smell that he had. It was during this time of great sorrow that my husband did the loveliest thing. He had found three container candles that spelled out S-A-M—one for *S*, one for *A*, and one for *M*. On each candle's container, there were words that started with that letter. For *S*, the words were *strong*, *special*, and *superstar*. *A* was for *adventurous*, *active*, *affectionate*, and *adorable*. The *M* stood for *mighty*, *marvellous*, and *miracle*. He put them down and lit them, and it became our little memorial to Sammie. I love candles, but to see these candles spell out his name and also include words that reflected how Sammie was, I was touched. Every night for weeks, I lit those candles with their vanilla aroma and thought of Sammie. Then one night, the candle wax had burned down so far that the wicks wouldn't light anymore. So I took the three candle containers and placed them in a special place, and every now and then, I look at them and remember Sammie, for the wonderful pet he was, and my husband, for the wonderful man he is.

As with Towser before him, we got Sammie cremated and his ashes came home to my parents' place in a teal blue urn, which now sits on a shelf in their house with a photo of Sammie beside it. Towser's ashes were buried under a beautiful red rose bush in my parent's garden. I like the thought that both dog's ashes are with my parents. Along with the urn, the pet crematorium gave us a laminated story (author unknown) called "Rainbow Bridge" which reads the following:

> Just this side of heaven is a place called Rainbow Bridge. When an animal dies that has been especially close to someone here, that pet goes to Rainbow Bridge. There are meadows and hills for all of our special friends so they can run and play together. There is plenty of food, water and sunshine, and our friends are warm and comfortable.
>
> All the animals who had been ill and old are restored to health and vigour. Those who were hurt or maimed are made whole and strong again, just as we remember them in our dreams of days and times gone by. The animals are happy and content, except for one small thing; they each miss someone very special to them, who had to be left behind.

They all run and play together, but the day comes when one suddenly stops and looks into the distance. His bright eyes are intent. His eager body quivers. Suddenly he begins to run from the group, flying over the green grass, his legs carrying him faster and faster.

You have been spotted, and when you and your special friend finally meet, you cling together in joyous reunion, never to be parted again. The happy kisses rain upon your face; your hands again caress the beloved head, and you look once more into the trusting eyes of your pet, so long gone from your life but never absent from your heart. Then you cross Rainbow Bridge together . . . .

I'm such a sook that I still get teary-eyed when I read it. My grief over the loss of Towser and later Sammie was the same—all encompassing. I almost didn't want to get Max because I knew that one day I would have to go through the grief again with him when his time came, and I didn't know whether I could bear it. The thought that got me through was that both Towser and Sammie lived good lives—they were well looked after and had shared in all of our family's happy moments. They had shared a lot of fabulously crazy moments with us as well. But most importantly of all, they knew they were loved. My parents and I loved them with our whole hearts and to our fullest capacities, and I'm convinced Towser and Sammie felt that magical energy every day of their lives. They would have seen the smiles that came on our faces when we saw them and would have felt the care that went into our hugs and pats. That's really all that's important.

The gifts that all of my boxers have given, I would never change for the world. Even though owning a pet ends in sadness when they move on, the sheer joy, happiness, companionship, devotion, and love that they bring to your life is worth every second of grief. It is better to have had and lost than never to have had. Towser and Sammie lived full lives—as Max does now—and I can only hope that I will be able to feel the same about my life when I'm at the end of my days.

ANGELA LEMANIS

There's So Much More to Learn

L AST LESSON FOR now, and it's beautifully simple in its brevity: there is so much more for me to learn!

Whilst the life lessons in the preceding chapters were taught to me by three slightly crazy boxer dogs, many other life lessons were taught to me by family and friends who've had a lot to do with my personal growth to date. The good thing about life is that you never stop learning. I know that there are so many more new experiences in store for me in the future, and I look forward to learning something special from them all.

My philosophy on life mirrors American writer William Arthur Ward's view that "the adventure of life is to learn. The purpose of life is to grow. The nature of life is to change. The challenge of life is to overcome. The essence of life is to care. The opportunity of life is to serve. The secret of life is to dare. The spice of life is to befriend. The beauty of life is to give." For me, learning from life means living it, tasting it, travelling it, sensing it, and absorbing it at every opportunity. But what do I know for sure? What are the truisms in my life as it stands now?

Well, I've learned that I don't trust people who laugh too long at their own jokes, I've learned that five minutes of sunshine can revive you; that love is what it's all about; that you should always be happy to see those you love; that life is indeed a journey, not a destination; that you've got to do your own growing in order to actually grow up; you've got to fall down and get up again several times; that Murphy's Law exists, and that's OK; that to love an animal buoys the spirit; that I do some of my best thinking in the shower; that if someone says, "remind me to . . ." most times I will forget unless I write it down; that people will show their true selves to you if you look closely enough; that most of what goes on is fluff but beneath the fluff is the real essence; that snap judgements are both good and bad (good when it's intuition speaking, and bad when its ego speaking); that no one gets through life without a few tears; and that life is one big learning curve. Sometimes you've got to be wrong to know how to be right. Sometimes you've got to go through some bad places to arrive in a good one. Sometimes you will only understand things if you give yourself the time and space to ponder.

I know that saying "you know?" to someone who doesn't understand what you're talking about is a completely redundant statement. I also know that repeating the same thing and saying it louder each time will not make someone understand what you're saying any quicker. I know that matching your facial expressions to your thoughts is only good if you're thinking good things.

I know that most of us are too harsh on ourselves and that realistic expectations when it comes to ourselves are rarely realistic. I know that we should be our own best friends and cut ourselves a break every now and then. I know that common sense isn't that common anymore. I know that just because it's written in the paper or broadcast on television doesn't always mean it's true, right, or accurate. I know that the worst days in my life don't matter when I come home to the warm welcome I get from Andrej and Max. I know that I adore looking at the faces of those I love so well—all the little intricacies, every wrinkle, and every nuance and mannerism—I have committed them all to memory. I know that if I can't look myself square in the eye in the mirror, then I've got some work to do.

I know that every person has some cross to bear during this lifetime, but I also know that there is magic everywhere around us if we look. I know that when you're born your heart is whole and untouched. Over the course of your life, there will be times when your heart gets fault lines and a few fractures; but I know that no matter how bad, it doesn't actually break because the kindness of others in your life heals the heart little by little. I know that there's more good in this world than bad. I know that you should take every opportunity to celebrate achievements, successes, birthdays, long summer days, time spent with loved ones and all of the wonderful things life has to offer. That laughter and sleep are the best medicines, and they're both free. That saying something genuinely nice to someone will always have an impact.

I know that lessons are learned when you're ready to learn them, that wisdom is realised when you can handle it, that we're all in different phases of life's journey, and age has nothing to do with it. I know that the lessons we need to learn most are the ones we find the hardest to get our head around. I know that wise people didn't become wise by accident—instead, they listened, paid attention, took everything in, and then decided which parts they wanted to keep and which parts could be dispensed with.

ANGELA LEMANIS

I know that a lot of it has to do with how you react to situations. Life is about perspective and perception—we see what we want to see, and we believe what we want to believe, like the optimistic Black Knight character (from my favourite movie *Monty Python and the Holy Grail*) who fights King Arthur to prevent him from crossing the bridge. King Arthur cuts off the Black Knight's left arm, and the knight says positively:

Black Knight: 'Tis but a scratch!
King Arthur: A scratch? Your arm's off!
Black Knight: No, it isn't!
King Arthur: Well, what's that then? (pointing to the knight's left arm which is now lying on the ground)
Black Knight: I've had worse.
King Arthur then cuts off the Black Knight's right arm.
King Arthur: Look, you stupid bastard. You've got no arms left.
Black Knight: Yes, I have.
King Arthur: Look! (pointing at the Black Knight's armless body)
Black Knight: It's just a flesh wound.

It just goes to show that perception is everything! Reality is only reality for us—a reflection of what we believe to be so. Trust yourself and listen to your intuition and always do what you feel is right for you.

I know that universal laws are potent and that balance is vital for health and happiness. I know that time can be both an enemy and a friend. I know that Karma is very real, so be careful what you put out into the world as it has a way of coming back.

I know that Max will continue to go out onto the back deck every night and sit "contemplating life" or whatever it is that he actually does out there. I know that I will continue to watch him, as he sits peacefully enjoying the solitude, and marvel at how in tune he is with his senses as he sits in the ambient twilight and soaks up the sights, smells and sounds that only that time of day can bring.

I know that the day your dog dies is a bad day. I know that I will be right there with Max when his time comes because I believe that even if it is difficult to watch, I want him to know that I'm with him and that he's not going to be alone at the end. He's going to have a friend with him to give him a pat and send him off on his next journey. I know that it's always hard to say good-bye to those you love, but I also know that time does heal all. Saying good-bye is not meant to be easy, but eventually you move from devastation to only remembering the good times. All you need to know is that you loved them and that they knew you did. The important thing is to never take anything for granted, expecting that it will always be there because it won't.

I know that I will always have a boxer dog in my life—even when I'm old. I know that I will continue to talk to my dogs because even though it might make me strange (yes, I know they can't understand what I'm saying), I'm convinced that they can tell how much I love them from my tone of voice. I know that I will take the lessons I've learned from each of my dogs and use them to grow as a person and a dog owner. I will do better as I continue to put my knowledge to work. I know there will be hard times ahead and that the path isn't always smooth, but I'm not frightened because I know that I'm stronger than I've previously given myself credit for.

I know that as Susan Kennedy said, "Dogs are miracles with paws," and that everyone should own at least one in their lifetime. I know that I want to be "as good of a person as my dog already thinks I am."

What I do absolutely know for sure is that of all my lessons learned to date, some of the most enjoyable and most meaningful were taught to me by three four-legged, wrinkly, slobbery boxer dogs to which I will forever be grateful. Thank you, Towser, Sammie, and Max for teaching me the wisdom that can only come from dogs.

What is a dog?

"He is your friend, your partner, your defender, your dog. You are his life, his love, his leader. He will be yours, faithful and true, to the last beat of his heart."—Unknown

AUTHOR BIO

ANGELA LEMANIS IS an award-winning public relations practitioner who has worked in consultancy and government roles in both Australia and New Zealand. Born and raised in Australia, Angela received a Bachelor of Journalism degree from James Cook University and a Graduate Certificate in Public Relations from the University of Southern Queensland. When she is not writing, Angela can be found hanging out with her husband Andrej and their crazy Boxer dog, Max. This is her first book.

CPSIA information can be obtained
at www.ICGtesting.com
Printed in the USA
LVOW12s1501211216
518248LV00016B/161/P